FREEMASONRY

FREEMASONRY

An Introduction

MARK E. KOLTKO-RIVERA, PH.D.

JEREMY P. TARCHER/PENGUIN
a member of Penguin Group (USA) Inc.
New York

JEREMY P. TARCHER/PENGUIN

Published by the Penguin Group

Penguin Group (USA) Inc., 375 Hudson Street, New York, New York 10014, USA •
Penguin Group (Canada), 90 Eglinton Avenue East, Suite 700, Toronto, Ontario M4P 2Y3,
Canada (a division of Pearson Penguin Canada Inc.) • Penguin Books Ltd,
80 Strand, London WC2R 0RL, England • Penguin Ireland, 25 St Stephen's Green,
Dublin 2, Ireland (a division of Penguin Books Ltd) • Penguin Group (Australia),
250 Camberwell Road, Camberwell, Victoria 3124, Australia (a division of
Pearson Australia Group Pty Ltd) • Penguin Books India Pvt Ltd, 11 Community Centre,
Panchsheel Park, New Delhi–110 017, India • Penguin Group (NZ), 67 Apollo Drive,
Rosedale, North Shore 0632, New Zealand (a division of Pearson New Zealand Ltd) •
Penguin Books (South Africa) (Pty) Ltd, 24 Sturdee Avenue,
Rosebank, Johannesburg 2196, South Africa

Penguin Books Ltd, Registered Offices: 80 Strand, London WC2R 0RL, England

The opinions and statements published herein are the responsibility of the author, and do not
necessarily represent the policies or views of the Masonic fraternity. No one speaks with final authority
regarding Freemasonry or its symbolism. This publication is not sponsored or endorsed by any Grand
Lodge, or any other Masonic organization.

Most Tarcher/Penguin books are available at special quantity discounts for bulk purchase for sales
promotions, premiums, fund-raising, and educational needs. Special books or book excerpts also can
be created to fit specific needs. For details, write Penguin Group (USA) Inc. Special Markets, 375
Hudson Street, New York, NY 10014.

Library of Congress Cataloging-in-Publication Data

Koltko-Rivera, Mark E. (Mark Edward), date.
Freemasonry : an introduction / Mark E. Koltko-Rivera.
p.   cm.
Originally published: [Winter Park, Fla.] : LVX Pub. Co., 2007.
ISBN 978-1-58542-853-3
1. Freemasonry.   2. Freemasons.   I. Title.
HS395.K67   2011   2010032895
366'.1—dc22

Printed in the United States of America
3   5   7   9   10   8   6   4   2

BOOK DESIGN BY MEIGHAN CAVANAUGH

While the author has made every effort to provide accurate telephone numbers and Internet addresses
at the time of publication, neither the publisher nor the author assumes any responsibility for errors,
or for changes that occur after publication. Further, the publisher does not have any control over and
does not assume any responsibility for author or third-party websites or their content.

CONTENTS

. . .

Frontispiece to the 1784 edition of James Anderson's *Constitutions of the Ancient Fraternity of Free and Accepted Masons*, edited by John Noorthouk, and published in London by J. Rouza, by order of the Grand Lodge of Freemasons in that city. The plate was drawn by Giovanni Battista Cipriani and Paul Sandy and engraved by Francesco Barolozzi and James Fittler. The *Constitutions*, first published in 1723, publicized the legendary history of Freemasonry, which purportedly stretched back for centuries; this history has much symbolic significance.

The frontispiece portrays a symbolic or allegorical scene set in London's Freemasons' Hall; the architectural detail seems to be accurate. In the eighteenth century, it was not uncommon for a book's frontispiece to show a tableau of allegorical figures, such as we see here. The uppermost figure, Truth, holds a mirror that reflects rays of light (presumably from heaven) onto items that one would see in a Masonic lodge of the day, such as the globes of the world and the sky, seen on the table. Truth is accompanied by Faith, Hope, and Charity (right to left). The "Genius" (teaching spirit) of Freemasonry descends into the hall with the lighted torch of knowledge; the Genius of Freemasonry also carries a ribbon with a medal hanging from it, to give to the Grand Master of Freemasons as a token of divine approval.

(See description of the frontispiece on the website of the Grand Lodge of British Columbia and Yukon at http://www.freemasonry .bcy.ca/texts/gmd1999/tb04.html.)

. . .

To my Masonic forebears:

F. Leland Watkins, Sr.   F. Leland Watkins, Jr.
(1869–1958)   (1899–1985)

Master Masons
32°, Masters of the Royal Secret
Knights Templar

Presidents of the Dakota Business College
Masonic leaders in Fargo, North Dakota

Great-grandfather and Grandfather of
Kathleen Koltko-Rivera
my loving and beloved wife

INTRODUCTION

In recent years, there has been a sharp increase in curiosity about Freemasonry. This has occurred for a variety of reasons, including the mention of Masonry in several best-selling books and popular movies. All of this exposure has led many people to wonder what Freemasonry is and whether there is something in Masonry for them. In my experience, a substantial number of these people newly interested in Freemasonry have a keen interest in the esoteric: they want to know what the rumored "mystery" of Freemasonry is all about, and what it means to their lives.

This short book is written for the man who is curious about Freemasonry, including the new Mason. (Standard Freemasonry is a male organization, but see Chapter 6.) In writing this book, I have tried to keep in mind the main issues that someone interested in Freemasonry might be thinking about: What is Freemasonry? Why do men become Freemasons, especially these days? What does it really mean to be a Freemason? How does Freemasonry work? What is the point of Masonic symbolism? How did Freemasonry begin? What about the controversies and even the scandalous rumors that one occasionally hears about Freemasonry? What about the depictions of Freemasonry that one sees in the movies or reads in books? How does one become a Freemason? What are reliable sources to consult in learning more about Freemasonry? These are my concerns here.

For the sake of the reader interested in the esoteric side of Freemasonry, I have paid special attention to the meaning of Masonic symbolism and how this is applied to Freemasons' lives. In addition, I carefully address the possible relationship between Freemasonry and the traditions of earlier days.

Something about Freemasonry has piqued your interest. Is Freemasonry for you? By the time you finish this book, you will know whether Freemasonry is something about which you wish to learn more. If you find that Freemasonry is *not* for you at this time, I thank you for your interest, and I bid you the best of good fortune in your journey through life. If you find that Freemasonry *is* of further interest to you,

I am glad for your interest; however, you will need to take further action to satisfy your desire for more information.

In the United States, Freemasons are generally prohibited by Masonic custom from inviting someone to become a Freemason. Therefore, if you find that you are interested in Freemasonry, you will need to take the initiative yourself to seek out a lodge and apply for membership. This book will tell you how to do that.

I am a Freemason. I believe in Masonic values. Freemasonry has contributed to the quality of my life in several ways. Even more important, I feel that Freemasonry has contributed to the good of society in several ways, over the course of centuries. For these reasons, I feel that it is worthwhile to publish accurate information about the Masonic fraternity. This edition features well over 50 percent more material than the earlier edition published by LVX Publishing. The glossary near the end of the book may help make the terminology of Freemasonry less confusing.

I am grateful for the generous guidance and assistance rendered to me by Thomas M. Savini, the director, Roseann M. Huschle, receptionist, and Catherine Walter, curator, at the Chancellor Robert R Livingston Masonic Library of Grand Lodge, the jewel in the crown of New York Freemasonry. I obtained access there to valuable materials I could have found in no other library in the state. I am also grateful for the use of materials held by the Elmer Holmes Bobst Library of New York University. I am particularly grateful for materials generously shared by Arturo de Hoyos.

I thank Kathleen Koltko-Rivera, Arturo de Hoyos, and Viktor Koltko for their comments on an earlier version of this manuscript. I am thankful to many at Tarcher/Penguin for helping to make this book a reality, such as Gabrielle Moss, Jennifer Tait, Jennifer Uram, and Balie Keown. I am particularly grateful to Mitch Horowitz, my editor at Tarcher/Penguin, for his vision, which has brought this work to a larger public, and for his manner, which made this new author very comfortable.

1.

Freemasonry: What It Is

The question "What is Freemasonry?" has been answered many ways over the last three centuries. It is not easy to answer, because our society has very few examples of similar organizations for comparison. However, this is an important question for several reasons: Freemasonry is important in the lives of millions of people today; during the course of over three centuries, modern Freemasonry has inspired countless people; and Masonry has shaped the ideals of nations, including the United States of America.

Here is a brief definition that packs a lot of meaning into just a few words: **Freemasonry is a fraternity that uses ceremonies of initiation to teach symbolic lessons about**

philosophy, morality, and character. Now let us unpack this definition, phrase by phrase.

"Freemason is a fraternity . . .": Masonry is open to adult men of good character who believe in a Supreme Being. It is built around the ideas of the development of character, personal growth, responsibility, duty, service to God and humanity, and fellowship.

"Freemasonry . . . uses ceremonies of initiation . . .": In brief, initiation is a ritual activity through which people are imparted certain teachings confidentially, are made part of a group, and become people who are in some way different from who they were before initiation. A Masonic initiatory ceremony is called a "degree"; there are three of them in basic Freemasonry. (More about degrees later.)

Through the initiatory experiences of Freemasonry, a man learns certain truths in a dramatic fashion. He also obtains membership within the international fraternity of Masonry. The new Mason learns certain signs by which he can identify himself as a Mason to other brothers whom he meets in his travels, even if these travels take him around the world. In addition, the new Mason places himself under obligation to keep these signs of recognition secure and to live according to certain high ideals.

In many cultures throughout history, and for many generations, initiatory experiences were a part of life for adults of good character; unfortunately, in modern life in the industrialized world, opportunities for real initiation are few. By contrast, Masonry's ceremonies of initiation have a history measured in centuries. (I say more about initiation in the next chapter.)

"Ceremonies . . . [that] teach symbolic lessons about philosophy, morality, and character": Within the initiatory experiences of Freemasonry, a man is exposed to many symbols that offer insight into several important issues: how men should live, toward what ends they should direct their efforts, the way in which people should relate to one another, and their relationship to God.

This is Freemasonry. It conveys initiatory experiences to today's man, giving him a context in which to reflect upon his roles and his life in contemporary society.

DIFFERENT PERSPECTIVES ON FREEMASONRY

There are other ways to look at Freemasonry. One can look at it as an organization, a social fellowship, a place of ritual and symbolism, and a vehicle for spiritual growth.

Freemasonry as an Organization

The Masons of a given community are organized into one or more groups called lodges. Lodges get together, typically once or twice per month, in regular meetings called Stated Communications; additional meetings, called Special Communications, are held as necessary to conduct initiatory rituals. The lodge also offers opportunities to socialize and to give service to the community.

In the United States, the lodges within each state are organized into a Grand Lodge. The Grand Lodge is the highest administrative unit within Freemasonry; its Grand Master (who serves a term of one to three years) is its highest authority. There is no national, centralized authority for American Freemasonry; there is no international, centralized authority for global Freemasonry, either.

Freemasonry as a Social Fellowship

A given lodge includes men from many different walks of life: tradesmen, office workers, professionals, civil servants, retirees, students. Masonry is thus an opportunity to become fellows with men of different social, religious, and political backgrounds. Masons do not discuss sectarian religious issues or partisan politics at the lodge. Lodge activities are an opportunity to make friends with many different kinds of people.

FREEMASONRY AS A PLACE
OF RITUAL AND SYMBOLISM

The opening and closing ceremonies of regular meetings, and the special ceremonies of initiation, are opportunities for Freemasons to enact ritual. These ceremonies, in turn, use symbolism to convey teachings about our search for truth, our journey through life, and our relationship to the Divine.

In this book, I do not discuss the specifics of Masonic rituals; the actual content of the rituals is something that Masons keep confidential. However, anyone who has actually experienced these rituals can assure you from personal experience that there is nothing in these rituals of a blasphemous or degrading nature. Rather, the initiatory rituals of Freemasonry are dignified ceremonies of high drama that impress upon the candidate, through symbolism, the importance of the search for enlightenment, moral behavior, honor, and commitment.

FREEMASONRY AS A VEHICLE
FOR SPIRITUAL GROWTH

Freemasonry is a part of one's life, not just something that happens in the lodge. There is much to study, much to ponder, and much to practice as one seeks to embody the ideals and lessons taught in the symbolism of Freemasonry. Over time, the practice of ritual in the lodge, the study of Masonic literature, and personal reflections and experiences involving Masonry all stimulate development of character and spiritual growth.

WHAT FREEMASONRY IS NOT

It is also important to explain what Freemasonry is *not*. It is not a religion, nor a way to gain power or status within the community, nor a conspiracy to rule the world. Because Masonry has been accused of being each of these things, this matter is worth considering in more detail.

FREEMASONRY IS NOT A RELIGION

Freemasonry focuses on moral behavior and spiritual concerns, but is not itself a religion. Masonry uses many spiritual symbols (such as altars, and the "Volume of Sacred Law") and actions (such as prayer); in this, it is like the Boy Scouts of America (which conducts prayer at its meetings) or the justice system (some courts of which adminster oaths on a sacred text, often the Bible. However, Freemasonry offers no savior or plan for salvation; there is no priesthood or ministry within Freemasonry. Freemasonry is not opposed to these things, but it does not have any of its own to offer.

In fact, discussion of sectarian religious doctrines—like discussion of partisan politics—is banned from the lodge, so that men of different religious and political viewpoints can join together in peace and harmony. The entire extent of what one might call "doctrinal" teachings that are shared in the lodge are the concepts of: (a) the fatherhood of God, (b) the brotherhood of man, (c) the immortality of the soul, and (d) the obligation to live honestly, justly, and morally. These are fine principles, but they do not constitute a religion.

On the other hand, Freemasonry does *not* teach that all religions are the same, or that all religious doctrines are equally valid. Freemasonry simply says that it leaves all such questions to the conscience of the individual.

Freemasonry is not a path to power or status

Freemasonry is also not a vehicle to obtain social advantage, business profit, or political power. Men who are interested in such benefits must seek for them elsewhere. Candidates for the degrees of Freemasonry must specifically indicate that they are not influenced to enter Freemasonry by such motives.

Freemasonry is not a conspiracy

Freemasonry is also not a vehicle for political domination: Masons do not rule the world from behind the scenes, nor do they seek to do so. On most political issues, one will find Freemasons on both sides of the question. Even in the American Revolutionary War and in the Civil War, there were prominent Masons fighting on opposing sides.[1]

Masons *do* seek to advance the causes of religious and political liberty, as well as public education, but they do this openly and personally, in their capacity as private citizens,

---

1. Halleran (2010) relates historically accurate accounts of Masonic fellowship extended across Civil War battle lines.

rather than as Masons. This is because Freemasonry itself does not become involved in partisan politics.

"But What About the 'Mysteries'?"

The reader might wonder about the so-called mysteries of Masonry. There have been rumors for centuries alleging that Masons have access to hidden knowledge. Are there Masonic mysteries? Yes and no.

In terms of the "outer" mysteries—truths about political conspiracies, the locations of treasures, the site of Atlantis—Masonry has nothing to offer. As a group, Masons know nothing about these subjects.

On the other hand, Masonry offers knowledge of the *inner* mysteries through its initiations and symbolism. The symbols of Masonry teach lessons involving philosophy, morality, and ethics. There is much in Masonry that can help a man address the larger questions of life.

In the so-called higher degrees of Freemasonry, Masons are exposed to a variety of esoteric traditions. Some degrees convey traditions about the temple built by Solomon, the ancient king of Israel, or the medieval Knights Templar. Others expose the Mason to the esoteric teachings of the Kabbalists, alchemists, Rosicrucians, and so on. Here too, the focus is on inner development.

Symbols, ancient wisdom about God and man, inner development: these are the mysteries of Masonry. If these are the sorts of mysteries that interest you, then you may find much of value in Freemasonry.

MASONIC SECRECY

Masonry has not only mysteries, but actual *secrets*: its signs of recognition and its initiation ritual. Masons swear oaths with penalties (purely symbolic) to keep these secrets. Why keep these confidential, especially when they are described in published exposures available in libraries and bookstores?

Masonic secrecy—or, as I prefer to call it, Masonic privacy—is a way to maintain a connection to centuries of tradition. In addition, some Masons believe that the signs of recognition are descended from the practices of the fugitive Knights Templar, who were on the run after being falsely accused of blasphemy by a corrupt king in the Middle Ages (see Chapter 5).

Beyond that, initiation is meant to have an effect on the mind. That effect is mitigated when one knows all the details in advance. There is a point in receiving initiation as it was composed: one step at a time.

There is also a point to introducing today's man to the notion that one should *keep one's word*—even on seemingly small things. Keeping Masonic secrets has little obvious consequence, but it teaches an important lesson.

SUMMARY

Freemasonry is a fraternity that uses ceremonies of initiation to teach symbolic lessons about morality, character, and philosophy. It is a social fellowship, a place for ritual and symbolism, and a vehicle to assist in spiritual growth. However, it is not a religion, a path to social advantage or political power, nor a conspiracy to rule the world. The mysteries of Masonry involve the inner world, not the outer world. Masonic secrecy connects men to centuries of tradition and has a symbolic purpose.

2.

Why Men Become Freemasons

Why would today's man become a Freemason? As it happens, there are many reasons why a man of the twenty-first century might be interested in this venerable fraternity.

The twenty-first century has much to offer. The Internet gives instant access to an immense volume of information, and virtually instantaneous worldwide communication with billions of people is possible. Nanotechnology promises to revolutionize manufacturing and health care. Genetic technology has already begun to transform medicine. Our opportunities for recreation and entertainment have no parallel in the history of humankind. The ordinary middle-class person has a higher quality of life than the kings of the Middle Ages.

However, in the midst of all this technological power, it is abundantly clear that there is much that is lacking in the world of the twenty-first century. Consider the following:

- Modern communication technology allows us to be in contact with people around the world instantly. However, never before has the world seen so much conflict: groups spread hate about other groups on the Internet, along with directions for developing weapons of mass destruction to carry out their agenda.

- Domestically, American society suffers from a breakdown in civility. This is evident in many areas. For example, in everyday social intercourse, there has been a noticeable coarsening of public manners over the last generation. Much of what constituted civilized behavior has been abandoned, in manners, dress, and language.

- American popular culture is highly materialistic, as shown by the national obsession with celebrity, fame, and wealth. These concerns betray a spiritual emptiness in much of our society and lead to psychological unhealthiness and unhappiness.[2]

- Whether we consider the global environment, the

2. Kasser (2002).

threat of war, or the enduring crises of poverty and hunger, it is clear that our technological *knowledge* far exceeds our *wisdom*.

- In the United States, it seems clear that we are more socially isolated than ever before, yet we do not know what to do about it. This is especially the case among men of this generation, who have fewer close friends than men of earlier eras.

Freemasonry provides ways to address each of these issues. It is a fraternity that crosses political, religious, ethnic, and national boundaries. It instills in men a focus on civility and the development of wisdom. These are the sorts of things that many men of the twenty-first century are looking for. I do not mean to imply that Freemasonry is a panacea, because it is not—but it *is* a way to respond productively to the challenges of life in today's world.

In the rest of this chapter, I explain what Freemasonry has to offer the man of the twenty-first century. First and foremost, Freemasonry presents an opportunity for today's man to enter a centuries-old initiatic tradition and to enhance his knowledge of the world though the consideration of powerful symbols and teachings. Freemasonry is a vehicle for personal development. Masonry offers opportunities for fellowship, participation in ritual, and service.

FREEMASONRY AS AN INITIATIC TRADITION

The most distinctive features of Freemasonry include its rituals of initiation. However, in today's world, it is easy to misunderstand what "initiation" really is. Here, I will describe briefly what initiation is, how it has been expressed in various cultures throughout history, and how Freemasonry is part of "the initiatic tradition."

WHAT INITIATION IS

As the Sufi mystic Hazrat Inayat Khan put it, initiation "means a step forward, a step which should be taken with hope and courage."[3] There are several aspects to initiation in its comprehensive sense:

- Initiation marks a change from one state of life into another. The very word "initiation" comes from the Latin word *initium*, meaning "entrance" or "beginning." In this aspect, initiation may involve a transition in stage of life, for example, from youth to young adulthood, or from young adulthood to maturity. Or

---

3. Khan (1997), p. 101.

initiation may involve a transition to living under a different, "higher" set of rules. Some initiations involve both types of transition.

- Initiation involves the transmission of knowledge or instruction to the new initiate. Often, this knowledge is only available through the initiatory experience; this particular knowledge is not made available to people who are not initiated. The knowledge may involve spiritual principles, history, allegory, and symbolism.

- Initiation may involve the transmission of means of recognition, whereby one initiate may know that another person has been initiated.

- Initiation marks the entrance of the initiate into a special group or society.

- Initiations involve some kind of challenge, trial, or ordeal, whereby the candidate for initiation proves himself worthy of receiving the initiation.

- Initiation involves the making of ritual agreements involving the preservation of the secrecy and sacredness of the initiatory experience.

One can find "initiations" in modern society that have one or a few of these characteristics. For example, college fraternity "initiations" may involve a sort of ordeal—often quite humiliating—through which the candidate for fraternity membership must pass. However, in its original sense, there are very few examples of comprehensive initiatory experiences in Western society today.

INITIATION THROUGHOUT HISTORY

Initiatory rituals have been known from the most ancient times. To focus on Western civilization, there may have been initiatory rituals in ancient Egypt. This is suggested by the ancient Greek historian Herodotus, who implied that he had received initiation in Egypt.[4] Certainly in later Egyptian history we note the rise of the mysteries of Serapis.[5] The Eleusinian Mysteries of ancient Greece, perhaps the most important of the various Greek initiatory experiences, were conferred for two thousand years, until about AD 396; the Greeks also observed the mysteries of Orpheus.[6] One may find traces of Gnostic initiations dating from the third or

---

4. Herodotus, *The Histories*, Book II, paragraphs 170–171. A contrary perspective is offered by Nagel (1978).

5. Schmitt (1978).

6. See Otto (1978) and Schmitt (1978) for the Eleusinian mysteries, Wili (1978) for the Orphic mysteries, Burkert (1985) for both.

fourth century AD.[7] Some claim to find initiatory experiences offered as parts of various movements within Judaism,[8]
Christianity,[9] and Islam (the last, specifically within Sufism[10]).
Initiation has been a part of human cultures for a long time,
perhaps for most of recorded history.

Anthropologists have documented initiatory traditions
alive today among tribal peoples. However, with a few ex-
ceptions, most examples of the initiatic tradition have become extinct within Western civilization.

Freemasonry is an exception, and has offered initiation
to interested men for centuries. The relationship of Masonic
initiation to that of earlier cultures is a matter of debate
among Masonic historians. However, it is clear that Freemasonry does address many of the same issues as the earlier

---

7. Consider the Gnostic Sethian literature in the collections that have emerged
in recent years concerning the documents found at Nag Hammadi in Egypt,
such as Meyer (2007); to start, see Turner (2007).

8. The Qumran community of Jews in the first century AD practiced rituals
of initiation and purification; see the index of Vermes (2004) under the en-
tries for "initiation into the sect" and "purity and purification." The Hekhalot and Merkavah mystics of Palestine and Babylon, from the first century
BC to the tenth century AD, had practices that seem initiatory; see Scholem
(1974; 1978, ch. 2) and Dan (1993).

9. Nibley (1966), analyzing literature emerging after the days of the apostles,
concluded that the first Christians themselves had confidential initiatory
rituals that have since been lost to history.

10. Khan (1997).

traditions of initiation: the search for knowledge, conveyed through ritual and ceremony.

INITIATION IN FREEMASONRY

Masonic initiatory rituals have their roots in several traditions, including the initiatory ceremonies of medieval European stonemasons and legends about the ancient temple built by Solomon. The three basic initiatory ceremonies of Masonry—the first three "degrees"—have each of the marks of initiation mentioned earlier.

The three foundational degrees of Freemasonry follow the initiate in a symbolic journey from a state of ignorance to that of being an apprentice craftsman; then to the state of a "fellow of the craft," or journeyman; then to the state of a master of the craft. (Thus, the first three degrees of Freemasonry are named Entered Apprentice, Fellow Craft, and Master Mason.) This follows the progression of a medieval European craftsman. Along the way, the initiate learns lessons appropriate for each stage of life. Although Freemasons now confer the three basic degrees of initiation over the course of several months rather than many years, the degrees provide a framework to enhance the development of a man from youth through maturity.

Throughout the first three degrees of Masonry, the initiate learns principles to elevate his relationship with his fellows and with God. Freemasonry presents a system of ethics that gives the initiate a higher, more refined standard to live up to than that which is followed by the world at large.

Freemasonry presents its initiates with knowledge through the use of symbolism. These symbols have layers of meaning that invite private contemplation and study to learn their implications and applications. Some symbols involve spiritual and moral principles; some involve mythic history and allegory. All have application to the initiate's life. Freemasonry is not a religion, but it does present ethical and moral lessons through its ceremonial initiations. The principles and symbolism presented in these initiations can go a long way toward helping a man deal with the big questions of life.

In the Masonic initiatory ceremonies, initiates are taught symbolic means of recognition whereby a Mason can identify himself to lodges throughout the world. To enter Freemasonry is to enter the world's oldest and largest existing fraternity; one may visit lodges of Masonic brothers throughout North, Central, and South America, as well as in most of the countries of Europe, many Asian and African nations, and Australia.

For example, consider my "mother lodge" (the place where I became a Mason), in Florida. Within the twelve-month period after I was initiated, this lodge received Masonic visitors from many of the United States, a brother from Scotland, an entire deputation from Ireland, and brothers from England and Brazil. A friend from my Florida lodge visited a Masonic lodge in the Czech Republic. Now that I attend Masonic meetings in New York City, not a meeting goes by that I do not meet someone visiting from abroad. Freemasonry is a truly international fraternity.

The Masonic degrees involve moments of high drama and a sense of mystery. Although there are symbolic ordeals, there is no hazing, and certainly nothing remotely resembling torture. Masonic initiates take upon themselves obligations to preserve the confidentiality of the initiation ceremonies and our means of recognition.

SYMBOLS AND TEACHINGS

Symbols are more than simply signs. For example, the sign ☎ means that a public telephone is near, or that a string of digits is a telephone number; it does not mean more than that. A symbol, however, may have a depth of meaning, and layers of meanings, that become apparent to the searching mind over the course of years. These meanings, in turn, reveal some principle, some guideline for a good life, even some aspect of reality.

Some of the dozens of symbols of Freemasonry are well-known to the public, such as the square and compasses. What is *not* so widely known, however, is that each of these symbols has meaning, often layers of meaning. Masonry's many symbols have relevance to ethics, morality as broadly defined, and other important topics.

Many of the symbols in the first three degrees of Free-masonry are taken from the tools and customs of medieval European stonemasons. A fully initiated Freemason—that is, a Master Mason—is eligible to petition for membership in other orders of Freemasonry, such as the York Rite and the Scottish Rite; here symbols are found from other traditions as well.

A VEHICLE FOR SELF-DEVELOPMENT

It has often been noted that Freemasonry "seeks to make good men better." Freemasonry acts as a vehicle for self-development in several ways.[11] The precepts and principles

---

11. An extensive consideration of Freemasonry as a psychological system for inner development is given by MacNulty (1991), pp. 15–32.

taught in Masonry have an impact on how one conducts one's life. The responsibilities that one takes on within one's local lodge develop one's leadership abilities. The study of Masonic symbolism, philosophy, and history can broaden one's intellectual capacities. Participation in a "society of gentlemen" ultimately can make one more of a true gentleman in one's behavior, speech, dress, and manners.

FELLOWSHIP

Freemasonry is a social experience. Men today seem to have fewer friends than men of earlier generations. At lodge, or in other affiliated groups, Masons meet with other men from many different occupations, social backgrounds, religious and political beliefs, and walks of life. Some of these men become friends for life—friends who otherwise would not have met.

RITUAL

In a sense, a ritual is a symbol that is acted out in behavior, rather than being written or carved. Participation in ritual can have a powerful effect on the mind, teaching important lessons, even molding character.

Freemasonry is noteworthy for its ritual. The three basic degrees of initiation are highly ritualized and quite dramatic. Regular lodge meetings open and close with ritual. Additional rituals are used in the degrees of the Scottish and York Rites. Freemasonry presents many opportunities for the interested person to participate in meaningful ritual. There are not too many such opportunities in today's society.

SERVICE

Freemasonry offers many opportunities for meaningful service. This might involve service directly to needy individuals, service to the local community, or service to the brothers of the lodge itself.

Lodges differ in the projects in which they are involved. Lodge members are called upon to visit the sick, and to help widows and orphans (who may or may not have had a connection to a Mason). A lodge may build a community by collecting supplies for local schools, or helping at a function for a nonprofit group (like a community theater). In addition, lodges always offer the opportunity to serve as officers or committeemen in the lodge itself; often there are opportunities to serve as advisers to Masonic youth groups. Each of the organizations that build upon basic Freemasonry as a foundation—the York and Scottish Rites and the affiliated and "fun" organizations—have designated charities, service projects, and opportunities to serve as officers and committeemen as well.

SUMMARY

There are many reasons why the man of the twenty-first century might wish to become a Freemason. In its own way, Masonry addresses many areas in which today's world is lacking, as shown by the superficial approach to life seen in several areas of popular culture.

Freemasonry presents an opportunity to enter a tradition of personal initiation where a man can be exposed to symbols with layers of meaning and significance. These symbols, and the teachings of Freemasonry, provide insight into practical questions of life and conduct, as well as some of the larger questions of life.

The initiatory experience has several aspects: it marks a life transition; it transmits knowledge to the initiate; through some sort of challenge, it brings him into a special society with its own signs of recognition, which are kept secure through ritual agreements. The initiatic tradition can be traced through many cultures and centuries. Today,

Freemasonry offers a true initiatic experience to those who seek this path to self-development.

Freemasonry is a vehicle to develop the self, and to go beyond selfish concerns, through service and ritual. Freemasonry certainly provides many opportunities for fellowship. From the young adult to the retiree, today's man may well find Freemasonry to be of interest as a centuries-old fraternity for the twenty-first century.

3.

How Freemasonry Works

How does Freemasonry work? In this chapter, I describe what Masons do on a day-to-day basis; the organizational structure of Freemasonry; some of the values of Freemasonry; and, what it really means to be a Mason in terms of "the inner man."

AN EVENING AT
SOLOMON'S LODGE #987

Ed Tyler leaves home at about 7:00 P.M. He has already had dinner at home with his wife and children, cleaned up after dinner, and given everyone a kiss good-bye. In fifteen minutes, he is at the building where the Masons in his community meet. His local group of Masons calls itself Solomon's Lodge #987.[12]

The building is already full of members who have come early to socialize; Ed has come later than most, but he still has time to visit with a few of his many friends at the lodge. He is particularly happy to see three men who entered Freemasonry as initiates on the same night that he did: Wayne the film school instructor, Leroy the businessman, and Raymundo the sheriff's deputy. Ed had never met these fellows before their initiation; now, two years later, they were some of his closest friends.

This was the first of the two regular lodge meetings of the month. Solomon's Lodge has a monthly dinner, but that dinner will be before the second meeting of the month, two weeks from now. However, the first meeting of the month was special in a different way: the Master of the lodge designated this meeting as the one where officers of the lodge were to attend in tuxedos. Ed was Marshal of the lodge—the most junior of officers, the one who helped to welcome visitors to the lodge and so forth—and so Ed was here in his tux. As a young man, Ed had dressed in faded jeans and

---

12. Lodges are usually identified by a name and a number that are unique within a given state's Grand Lodge. There are many lodges named after King Solomon; I am not basing this description on any lodge in particular.

ripped T-shirts; now his tux was one of his favorite pieces of clothing, much to his wife's surprise and pleasure. The rest of the lodge dressed as usual, for the most part in dark jackets and ties.

After visiting with his friends for a while, Ed signed the lodge register on the "Marshal" line, entered the lodge room, went to the Marshal's chair, and put on a ceremonial apron embroidered with the symbol of the Marshal's office: a baton. (The apron is a distinctive piece of Masonic attire, worn by all Masons in the lodge room; see Figure 4-12 for an extraordinarily detailed example.) He also put on an ornate chain of office with the Marshal's "jewel" or badge (also a baton) suspended at the bottom, which fell to about the middle of his chest.

The other officers came in and assumed their stations. The chief officer, the Master of the lodge, sat in the East with the Senior Deacon and Chaplain; the Secretary, Treasurer, and Organist sat in the corners. The number-two man, the Senior Warden, sat in the West with the Junior Deacon and Marshal. The Junior Warden sat in the South with the two Stewards. The rest of the Lodge members took seats lining the northern and southern walls of the lodge room.[13]

---

13. The directions here—East, West, and South—are given in their Masonic sense: in *every* lodge room in the world, the chair where the Master sits is in

In the center of the lodge room was an altar, on top of which was a copy of what the Masons call the "Volume of Sacred Law." Tonight, as usual, the Volume of Sacred Law was represented by a large copy of the King James Bible, but recently the altar had also had upon it copies of the Jewish *Tanakh*, the Muslim *Qur'an*, the Hindu *Vedas*, a collection of Buddhist *sutras*, and the Latter-day Saints' *Book of Mormon*. As candidates of different religious backgrounds were initiated, each candidate was entitled to have open on the altar the volume that *he* held sacred.

At 7:30 P.M. sharp, the Master of the lodge—the Worshipful Master, as he was called (meaning "Respectful Master")—dropped his gavel and called the meeting to order. After the Pledge of Allegiance to the American flag, the lodge opened in ceremonial form, most of the major officers performing some duty to open the lodge in proper ritual form.

After the opening of the lodge, there was some business to attend to: visitors were introduced, announcements were read. Ed's favorite part of the meeting was Masonic Educa-

---

the (Masonic) East, and so on, regardless of the actual compass direction. Lesser lodge officers vary slightly across state jurisdictions; for example, New York lodges may have two Masters of Ceremonies, while Florida lodges have none.

tion, where a designated member of the lodge presented a lesson focused on some specific portion of the symbolic rituals of initiation; tonight's lesson involved the symbolic meaning of the square and compasses (see Chapter 4). After the Masonic Education lesson, there was a bit more business: petitions for membership were voted on, bills were paid. The Worshipful Master himself presented a brief lesson as well, regarding the true meaning of fellowship.

By about 9:30 P.M., the meeting was closed in ceremonial fashion, and afterward Ed socialized with his lodge brothers in the dining hall, over ice cream. The Senior Warden drafted Ed to take a specific part in the initiation ritual to take place at the next regular meeting of the lodge; Ed was glad to be involved. He also volunteered himself to the Chaplain to visit some lodge members who were in the hospital. Ed confirmed arrangements for the following week, when he, Wayne, Leroy, Raymundo, and a couple of other fellows from the lodge would have a night out, with buffalo wings, onion rings, and a lot of conversation on the menu. Then he was off, home to Kathy and the kids.

I have, of course, described a sort of ideal lodge. Real lodges show variations. Not all are as cosmopolitan as Solomon's

Lodge #987. There is a wide variety in the frequency with which lodges initiate candidates. Lodges also differ in the emphasis that they place on Masonic Education. Not everyone buys into a tuxedo policy, either. (Different strokes for different folks. I like the tuxes, myself.)

Different personal circumstances affect one's involvement with Freemasonry. Attendance at the once- or twice-monthly Stated Communications, along with the occasional ritual initiation, makes one an active Freemason. Ed has young children at home, which places serious demands upon his time. Someone older, whose children are grown—or someone younger or without children—might devote more time to other Masonic activities.

Other activities come in several flavors. First, one's own local lodge has other things going on than Stated and Special Communications. There may be formal service projects (for example, being a waiter at a charity dinner) and informal service projects (like painting a room at a widow's home). There may be social activities (like a holiday dinner). There is always committee work to do (for example, compiling the monthly newsletter). In addition, some brothers choose to work as officers. (Ed is the lodge Marshal—usually not a heavy job—but there are other offices with more responsibility.)

AFFILIATED GROUPS

Another flavor of activity involves different types of groups associated with Freemasonry. These are of three basic types: "the Rites," family groups, and "fun" groups.

THE RITES

One is never more of a Freemason than when one has received the third degree of initiation, Master Mason. However, there are other systems or collections of degrees—collections called "Rites"—that delve into different aspects of symbolism, some building upon the basic Masonic degrees, some going in other directions, some doing both. The two major Rites are the York Rite, a system of ten additional degrees, and the Scottish Rite, a system of twenty-nine additional degrees.

As the saying goes, "both Rites are right." Some Masons (such as this author) are active in both the Scottish and York Rites as well as the local lodge. Each group offers opportunities to learn symbolic rituals, ceremonies, and lessons; each group offers opportunities to serve in leadership capacities and to share fellowship with men from all walks of life. Each group also has a designated charity that it supports. (The York Rite charities include treatment for vision disorders. The Scottish Rite charities include treatment of language disorders in the Southern Jurisdiction and treatments for dyslexia or schizophrenia in the Northern Masonic Jurisdiction.)

GROUPS FOR FAMILY MEMBERS

There are groups for the family of a Master Mason. These include organizations for Master Masons and their spouses and female relatives (such as the Order of the Eastern Star, the Order of the Amaranth, the White Shrine of Jerusalem, and the Heroines of Jericho). There are Masonic youth groups: DeMolay International is for all young men, not just sons of Masons; Rainbow Girls is for all young women; Job's Daughters is for young women who are descendants of Master Masons. There are organizations for women (such as the Ladies' Oriental Shrine of North America, the Social Order of Beauceant, and the Daughters of Mokanna). Not all groups exist in all locations.

"FUN" GROUPS

Masonic "fun" groups also involve service and philanthropy. These include the Shriners and the Grotto, as well as other groups.

Fun groups emphasize socializing rather than ritual or education; their members may go on a cruise, for example. Fun groups also tend to put a strong emphasis on philanthropy and community service. The Shriners, for example, are famous for using their circus as a way to raise funds for their burn hospitals, which have everything but a cash register. (Patients are treated for free.) The Grotto supports programs for cerebral palsy research, dentistry for the handicapped, and so forth.

Different people have different interests and inclinations. Some Masons get involved with a number of affiliated groups, either to obtain further degrees, or to participate in groups with family members, or for fun; other Masons affiliate with only their local lodge. This matter is left entirely to the individual.

BEING A FREEMASON: THE INNER EXPERIENCE

It is fairly easy to learn the externals of Freemasonry: many details of the history; many of the symbols; the names and insignia of the officers, and so on. It is *not* so easy to learn, from reading, what it means to *be* a Freemason. This is a highly personal issue; to some extent, what it means to be a Freemason differs from Mason to Mason. However, despite these differences in individual perspective, one can discern some common themes.

Being a Mason means living by certain values. Not all Masons live up to all of these values; perhaps no one is a perfect example of all of them. However, these values are ideals to which many Masons aspire. As I understand them, these values include the following:

- Freemasons are engaged in a lifelong journey to light.
- Freemasons strive to walk uprightly and honorably before God and man.
- Freemasons strive to treat each other as brothers.
- Freemasons strive to conduct themselves as gentlemen in society.
- Freemasons reach out in service to their communities and society at large.
- Freemasons uphold religious tolerance.

Below, I discuss each of these values.

FREEMASONS ARE ENGAGED IN
A LIFELONG JOURNEY TO LIGHT

In the Masonic ceremonies of initiation, a recurring motif is the individual's search for light. Yet at no point in the rituals of initiation does the individual make a final arrival at light: the journey to light is lifelong.

Precisely what is meant by "light" is a matter for the individual Mason to ponder. It may be a spiritual, a philosophical, or a rational enlightenment, or all of these together. What is clear, though, is that the search for light is a major motivation in the Mason's life.

This is so different from the ways of the world at large. In modern Western society, at least as portrayed by the media, what is most valued is financial wealth, fame, and celebrity—and the faster these are attained, the better. In the face of this, Freemasonry puts forth a vision of continuing effort to attain inner wisdom. Different Masons pursue this vision in different ways: private study of different sorts, contemplation, practicing ritual degree work, or all of these; service itself can be an act of meditation. In any event, the search for light is explicitly a central aspect in the thoughtful Mason's life.

MASONS STRIVE TO WALK UPRIGHTLY AND HONORABLY BEFORE GOD AND MAN

The news media bring up scandal just about every day, involving some notable figures in every walk of life: celebrities in the entertainment world, sports, and the arts; business figures; politicians; prominent professionals; even religious leaders—every day, some of these people are revealed to have done something unseemly, even sordid, occasionally heinous. Of course, many people in these fields live upright lives, but the scandalous incidents one hears about some of these people—many of them role models in our society—are troubling, even discouraging.

By contrast, it is noteworthy that one of the most important Masonic values is to walk uprightly and honorably before God and man. Exactly what that means in any given situation is left up to the individual Freemason. Growth in Freemasonry involves developing one's moral conscience. For those Masons who are part of a specific religious tradition, this means living that religion as well as one can.

A central symbol in each Masonic lodge is a book called the Volume of Sacred Law; no Masonic lodge can conduct business without having the Volume of Sacred Law open on its altar. The Volume of Sacred Law is usually *represented* by a copy of the Bible, but it is understood that each

Mason must define for himself both what book or books define the Volume of Sacred Law for him, and how he is to understand and interpret its teachings. He is to live by the Volume of Sacred Law as well as he can, according to how he understands it.

However, this does *not* mean that anything goes. Masons choose what specific spiritual paths they shall follow; however, they are taught to *live* the paths that they choose, rather than to be followers in name only. All spiritual paths require a morally upright and honorable life, an enterprise that will require effort and sacrifice. That not every single Mason does this is no surprise; no movement is successful with all its nominal supporters. Nonetheless, honorable and upright living is the Masonic standard and aspiration.

FREEMASONS STRIVE TO TREAT EACH OTHER AS BROTHERS

The so-called reality shows on television emphasize competition, one-upmanship, even treachery in the name of success. Coalitions are temporary, backstabbing is common, and all efforts are directed to being the last man standing in one way or another.

By contrast, Freemasons are taught to treat each other as brothers. Every Mason is taught to be a brother to every other Mason; even someone who has received just the first degree of Freemasonry is thereafter referred to as "Brother so-and-so," rather than "Mister so-and-so." With that status of brotherhood come many obligations: to help a brother in need, to keep his confidences, to correct him gently if he errs, to work to spread brotherly feeling rather than an attitude of competition, to treat each other as members of a society of equals.

Many people have experienced the cliquishness of groups in the lunchroom at high school or the dining room at college. Sometimes these cliques are defined by ethnicity, sometimes by activity.

Freemasonry strives to transcend cliques. I am thinking of an informal late-night dinner that I attended with some of the members of my mother lodge. We invited every member of the lodge who could stay out a little later that evening. Around the tables of that restaurant were some men in law enforcement, a rocket engineer, a few businessmen, college students, and others. The group included men from African American, European American, and different Hispanic backgrounds. Several religious groups were represented, as were vastly differing educational backgrounds. The divisions of ethnicity, religion, education, and social class that so often mark social intercourse was conspicuously absent from our conversation. (I am pleased to say that I regularly have similar experiences with Masonic groups in New York City.)

I have gone to men like this privately for counsel on some personal matters; likewise, some of them have come to me. Freemasonry works to break down the barriers that separate good men, helping them to recognize that they are brothers, and to act the part.

FREEMASONS STRIVE TO CONDUCT THEMSELVES AS GENTLEMEN IN SOCIETY

The erosion of politeness and manners in public have been commented on by many observers. In contrast to this, Freemasonry is a society of gentlemen—not in the European or Colonial sense of "landed gentry," but in the modern American sense of "a person of gentility and manners." Masons are taught to address one another with respect, and to conduct themselves with some dignity. Being a gentleman, inside and out: that is part of being a Mason.

In Masonry, much value is placed on carefully fulfilling one's duties and responsibilities. I shall illustrate this with an example.

I recall participating in the initiation ceremony of three

young men receiving the Entered Apprentice degree. For the evening, I stood in the office and station of the Junior Warden in the South; the man standing at the station of the Senior Warden in the West was the actual Senior Warden of the lodge, but the rest of the officers—including the brother taking the position of the Worshipful Master— were stand-ins, as is usually the case during degree ceremonies. (This policy gives the whole lodge a chance to share in the ritual work.)

We had all met over the weekend for an hour to practice the ceremony. Several of us spent time in private study to learn our individual parts. When the night came for us to conduct the actual ceremony, everything clicked: we knew our parts, we carried out our ritual responsibilities with dignity and even a touch of drama, things happened when they were supposed to. It was a great pleasure to participate, and our preparation had an effect on our degree candidates. This kind of concern with precision—pride in one's workmanship—spills over into one's everyday life.

FREEMASONS REACH OUT IN SERVICE TO THEIR COMMUNITIES AND SOCIETY AT LARGE

Freemasons reach out in different ways to be of service to their communities and to society. Masons reach out to individuals in need, particularly widows and orphans; this help is often given anonymously, either through an act of the lodge, or of one or more individual Masons who become aware of a need. Many lodges support some organization within their community (like a preschool) with financial help, supplies, or personal services. Local lodges, the statewide Grand Lodge, and affiliated Masonic organizations all have favorite charities that they support financially, such as the Masonic Medical Research Laboratory in Utica, New York. I have already mentioned some of the charities supported by the York and Scottish Rites and the Shriners. Being a Mason means having an orientation toward service.

FREEMASONS UPHOLD RELIGIOUS TOLERANCE

Intolerance for religious differences is a plague in international, national, and local politics. No one in a post-9/11 world needs to be told that religious extremism can be deadly. Even aside from terrorism, it is noteworthy that some political or religious leaders will defame political opponents because of religious differences.

In contrast, Freemasons do not focus on religious differences at all. Yes, a man may only be a candidate for Masonry if he holds a belief in a Supreme Being. However, there Freemasonry ends all inquiry into a candidate's beliefs. All discussion of sectarian religious issues, such as the superiority of one religion over another, is strictly forbidden in the lodge. Freemasonry makes the same privileges available to all men, regardless of their religious affiliations. In this, it is a remarkable example of religious tolerance to which the world as a whole could look as an example.

One year, my mother lodge's Worshipful Master was a Jew, and the Senior Warden a Southern Baptist; another year, the Worshipful Master was a Roman Catholic, and the Marshal a Latter-day Saint. One Muslim friend of mine is the Master of his lodge, while another is a leader in the local Scottish Rite organization. My first year in my mother York Rite Chapter, we discussed where to attend a religious service as part of our annual Religious Commitment observance; recently, the chapter had attended a nearby synagogue, and on this occasion we decided to attend services at a local Seventh-Day Adventist congregation. Freemasonry exemplifies religious toleration. In the twenty-first century, that is an all too rare and beautiful thing.

In a letter written to the Scottish Rite the month after his book *The Lost Symbol* was released, Dan Brown stated why he chose to focus on Freemasonry in his novel. As he put it: "In a world where men do battle over whose definition of God is most accurate, I cannot adequately express the deep respect and admiration I feel toward an organization in which men of differing faiths are able to 'break bread together' in a bond of brotherhood, friendship, and camaraderie."[14] (Thank you, Mr. Brown.)

SUMMARY

In this chapter, I have described how Freemasonry "works" in the life of the individual Mason. At the level of the local lodge, Freemasonry offers opportunities to participate in rituals of initiation, in various positions of responsibility and leadership, on committees, and in different types of service projects.

There are groups affiliated with Masonry that offer further opportunities for activity. There are other systems of ritual initiation, or degrees, offered by the Scottish Rite and York Rite. There are groups for family members. There are also Masonic groups for fun and socializing.

The inner experience of Freemasonry involves Masons bringing certain values into practice. These include engag-

---

14. *Focus—December 2009* (2009).

ing in a lifelong search for light, striving to "walk uprightly before God and man," striving to treat each other as brothers, striving to conduct themselves as gentlemen in society, reaching out in service to the community and to society at large, and upholding such values as religious tolerance. These are not just pretty but empty phrases to the Mason; they are a vivid part of a Mason's experience.

4.

Masonic Symbolism

Masonry is famous for its symbolism. These symbols are of various sorts, some more obvious as symbols, some less so. The famous square and compasses, for example, is obviously a symbol. On the other hand, consider the collection of items in Figure 4-1. To the casual observer, this might seem like a random collection of tools, a book, and some celestial bodies. However, each and every one of these items is a symbol that is employed within the first three degrees of Freemasonry (including the sword, the hilt of which is hidden behind the book).

FIGURE 4-1. A random collection of objects
or a set of Masonic symbols?

To go even further in this direction, consider Masonic secrecy, the practice where Masons do not discuss their signs of recognition—the passwords, grips, and so forth—with non-Masons. The practice of Masonic secrecy is a symbol, too: among other things, it symbolizes the importance that Masons place on keeping one's word. If one cannot keep a simple password secret, one is not ready to handle many of the more important tasks of life, tasks which can require a considerable degree of discretion and confidentiality.

In this chapter, I briefly consider some of the more obvious symbols of the first three, or Blue Lodge, degrees of

Freemasonry.[15] For many of these I offer my own interpretations. I caution the reader that no one, including myself, may render an authoritative interpretation of Masonic symbolism beyond what is given in the Masonic ritual itself.

THE SQUARE

Many of the symbols of the Blue Lodge are taken from the tools of the working stonemasons of medieval Europe. The square is one of these, as shown in Figure 4-2.

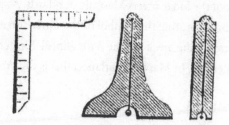

FIGURE 4-2. Some stonemasons' tools: the square, level, and plumb (left to right).

---

15. For reasons now lost to history, the foundational unit of Freemasonry, a lodge that confers the first three degrees of initiation, is referred to as a "Blue Lodge."

In the medieval era, the square was used to make sure that the corner of a building stone was perfectly "squared off" at a 90-degree angle, without unsightly bumps or gouges. This is a standard of precision that is challenging to meet in stonework. This standard is even more challenging when we consider the related moral meaning that Masonry gives to the square. In the task of building one's character, one needs to consider the perfection of one's work; one may well need to chisel off bad habits or character defects, or fill gaps in, say, one's social graces.

The square is also the symbol of office of the Worshipful Master of the lodge, who is responsible for making sure that the work of the lodge meets Masonic standards. A small medallion incorporating the symbol of the square on a chain is worn around the neck of the Worshipful Master during lodge meetings. In Masonic parlance, this is the Worshipful

FIGURE 4-3. The Masonic jewel of the Worshipful Master of a lodge: the square.

Master's "jewel" of office (see Figure 4-3). (Incidentally, in the majority of American lodges today, the arms of the square are of equal length.)

In addition, the symbol of a square shows up on the symbolic apron worn by the Worshipful Master. He may also wear, as unofficial Masonic "bling," a small pin of a square in his lapel.

THE LEVEL

The level (see the middle object in Figure 4-2) is a low-tech way of making sure that the top horizontal surface of a worked stone is perfectly flat. One places the level on a horizontal surface, and if the suspended ball on the string is *exactly* in the center of the semicircular opening at the bottom of the level, then you, as a stonemason, have created a perfectly flat surface. (These days, one would use a bubble-level, or even something with a laser beam.)

Within the lodge, the level signifies that all Masons are on the same "level" of distinction. A lodge may include a sanitation worker, the mayor, a law enforcement officer, an ice cream vendor, a college professor, a college student, a corporate president, a letter carrier, a small business owner, and a dog walker. All are equal in Masonry, and all are ad-

dressed the same way: "Brother." (Younger Masons occasionally address me as "Doctor," which is accurate but not
an appropriate title in Masonic contexts; I accept the com-
pliment, but encourage them to use "Brother.")

FIGURE 4-4. The Masonic jewel
of the Senior Warden of the lodge:
the level.

The level is also the symbol of office of the Senior Warden of the lodge (see Figure 4-4). This symbol also shows
up on his Masonic apron and perhaps on a lapel pin.

THE PLUMB

The plumb (see the right-hand object in Figure 4-2) is another low-tech tool used by medieval stonemasons. One
uses a plumb to make sure that a vertical surface of a worked
stone is perfectly straight, up and down. You take the plumb
and hold it up against the side of a stone. If the ball sus-

pended at the end of the string ends up *exactly* in the middle of the semicircular opening at the bottom of the plumb, then you, as a stonemason, have created a perfectly vertical surface.

Consider this as a message about one's conduct and speech, which should be honest, straight-shooting, guileless, and moral. We live in a world where a fair amount of

popular entertainment glorifies criminal behavior and betrayal. Freemasonry puts forth a very different idea about how one should conduct oneself, in public and private.

Incidentally, the plumb is also the symbol of office of the Junior Warden of the lodge. You can see an example of a Junior Warden's Masonic jewel in Figure 4-5.

FIGURE 4-5. The Masonic jewel of the Junior Warden of the lodge: the plumb.

THE COMPASSES

The compass—or "compasses"—was a medieval working stonemason's tool, used to "describe" (that is, to draw) circles. (See the compasses in Figure 4-1, with their fulcrum between the sun and the moon.) A nineteenth-century Masonic handbook explained the moral lesson of the compasses as follows:

> The Compass is a mathematical instrument used to describe circles. This we adopt as an emblem of prudence. It symbolically instructs us to put moral restraints on our appetites, to circumscribe within rational bounds, our wants, our pleasures, our expenses—warning us, that by an opposite course, we shall endanger our quiet, our health, our reputation, and our liberty.[16]

At various times in American history, we have celebrated the so-called virtues of excess. (I am thinking of the Roaring Twenties and the Go-Go Eighties of the twentieth century, as well as the ill-considered personal and corporate financial practices that led to the financial meltdown of 2008 and subsequent years.) The compass teaches us to keep the expression of our appetites and passions within due bounds. Not a popular message, perhaps—but a very wise one.

And yet, with the compass, we find that one layer of symbolism can be peeled back to reveal another layer or set of layers entirely (something that applies to all the symbols

---

16. Hardie (1818), p. 141, (formatting changed).

I have described thus far, incidentally). This is readily apparent when the compass is combined with the square, as I explain in the next section.

THE SQUARE AND COMPASSES

The square and compasses (Figure 4-6) is likely the most readily recognized sign of Freemasonry. Beyond that, it has its own symbolic significance. However, this is a significance that is not explicitly explained within the ritual of the three degrees of the Blue Lodge.

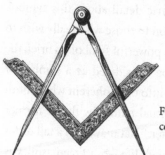

FIGURE 4-6. The square and compasses.

The nineteenth-century scholar of Masonic symbolism Albert Pike had this to say about the square and the compasses:

The square is an instrument that can be applied to level surfaces and rectilinear [that is, 90-degree] angles only. The earth anciently was supposed to be a level [that is, flat], with occasional inequalities of hills and valleys. . . .

The compasses are used to describe circles, and [are used] in spherical trigonometry in which the square cannot be used. They are therefore a fit symbol of the sky, the heavens, which form as it were, the roof of a half-sphere. . . .

The compasses, which are a fit symbol of the heavens, are also a fit symbol of all that is heavenly and spiritual; the square, which is a fit symbol of the earth, is also a fit symbol of all that is earthly and material, in nature and man.[17]

Pike goes into more esoteric detail about this symbol, and I commend his description to those who really wish to delve into the meaning of this powerful symbol. In brief, the square and compasses can be considered as a symbol of how the ideal man combines into one coherent whole both an earthly nature and a spiritual nature, with the former under the direction of the latter. That may seem a tall order to fill, in terms of directing one's life—but Freemasonry is not about taking the easy way.

---

17. de Hoyos (2008), pp. 95–97.

THE ALTAR, THE VOLUME OF SACRED LAW, AND THE TEMPLE BUILT BY SOLOMON

Within every Masonic lodge room there is an altar, be it a massive stone structure, a fine portable wooden item built for the purpose, or a card table pressed into service in an emergency. Upon that altar there is a book representing the Volume of Sacred Law, which must always be open and in the unobstructed view of the Worshipful Master whenever the lodge is in session. (This arrangement is shown in Figure 4-7, from the viewpoint of the Worshipful Master. If you look very closely, you will see, atop the Volume of Sa-

FIGURE 4-7. The Masonic Volume of Sacred Law atop the altar.

cred Law, the square and compasses—upside down from this point of view.)

All of this raises a question. Freemasonry is not a religion (as I explain in Chapter 7). What, then, is it doing with an altar?

The presence of the altar is likely connected to the fact that the Masonic lodge room itself represents the Temple built by King Solomon in ancient times. (A reconstruction of the temple is shown in Figures 4-8 and 4-9. Strictly speaking, the lodge room represents one portion or another

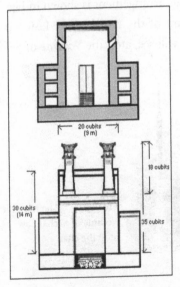

FIGURE 4-8. The Temple built by Solomon, viewed from the East (*top*, cutaway view; *bottom*, exterior view).

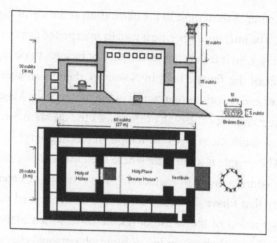

FIGURE 4-9. The Temple built by Solomon (*top*, cutaway elevation from the South; *bottom*, cutaway from above).

of the temple, depending upon the ritual work that is to be done at a given meeting.)

Temples have altars. A large altar for burnt offerings stood outside and to the east of the temple built by Solomon, and that is usually what people focus on when they hear about "the temple altar." However, inside the temple itself, near its very center, there was the *altar of incense*[18] (which you can see in

18. The construction of the original altar of incense, placed in the tabernacle by Moses centuries before Solomon built the temple, is described in the Bible

the center of the temple in the illustration at the top of Figure 4-9). The burning of incense is usually interpreted as a symbol of prayer. So it is that, just as the altar of incense stood in the center of the Temple built by Solomon, there is an altar for prayer and devotions that stands in the center of the Masonic lodge room. Of course, all of this raises the question, what is the symbolic meaning of the temple in Freemasonry?

The temple is a building where the Divine Being somehow connects with humankind.[19] The symbols of Freemasonry that I have described earlier are all items used in the construction of literal buildings, items to which Masonry gives the symbolic meaning of building personal character in one fashion or another. The ancient and external temple, then, is a model for something that Masons are to build within themselves: they are to make themselves appropriate abodes in which the Spirit of the Divine Being can dwell. As another interpretation, Masons are to use the symbolic tools to form themselves into perfectly shaped "stones," fit for use in a symbolic temple.

This is a grand, ambitious goal for human development.

---

in Exodus, chapter 30, verses 1–10. The construction of the equivalent altar of incense (the "golden altar") in the temple built by Solomon is mentioned in 2 Chronicles 4:19.

19. The idea of a temple, from the viewpoint of several cultures, is explored by Lundquist (1993).

In meeting that goal, the Mason is confronted continually with what is to be his guide, the Volume of Sacred Law, the Divine word itself—an important item atop the altar of Freemasonry.

THE LETTER *G*

Suspended over the altar or the chair of the Worshipful Master within the lodge room we see the letter *G*. This is shown in the stylized depiction of a lodge room that we see in Figure 4-10.

FIGURE 4-10. The letter *G* suspended over the altar in a Masonic lodge room.

On one level, this letter stands for "geometry," the science without which the medieval stonemasons could never have erected their cathedrals. On another level, it stands for "God," without whom there would have been no purpose to building those same cathedrals. (We are reminded that at least the Grand Lodge era of Freemasonry began in England, where the English language affords this happy coincidence in initial letters.)

Here we see a conjunction of reason and faith that shows up repeatedly within Freemasonry. On the one hand, the idea that "G is for Geometry" encourages us to take a rational approach to life; there is no more strictly rational science than mathematics, of which geometry is the visual expression. On the other hand, the idea that "G is for God" encourages us to consider the territory of faith, even mysticism, certainly devotion. In the world, some see these forces—reason and faith—as opposed. In the Masonic lodge, they are seen as complementary.

There is another place where the letter G shows up regularly in Masonry. This is in the middle of the square and compasses (Figure 4-11). This is probably the symbol that best stands, in many people's minds, for Freemasonry itself—although nowhere in Masonic ritual is this symbol defined as such.

(Incidentally, the square and compasses, with or without the letter G, is a registered trademark, or is copyrighted, in many jurisdictions.[20] Do not plan to brand your product, Masonic or not, with the square and compasses.)

FIGURE 4-11. The square and compasses with the letter G.

These are some of the symbols of the Blue Lodge. And yet this just scratches the surface of even just Blue Lodge symbolism, as we can see from Figure 4-12.

In Figure 4-12 we see a variety of Masonic symbols, mostly from the Blue Lodge, some of which I have described, and many of which I have not. The symbols are embroidered on a Masonic apron (itself a symbol I have not described here), one supposedly made by Madame Lafayette and given by General Lafayette to General George

---

20. *The Mason's Mark* (2007).

FIGURE 4-12. A Masonic apron, reportedly
presented by Lafayette to Washington.

Washington, perhaps America's most famous Mason, in
1784.[21] We see the square and compasses upon the Volume
of Sacred Law (somewhat like Figure 4-7, but from the
point of view of someone standing to the west of the altar,
rather than from the point of view of the Worshipful Master in the East). We also see a letter *G*, although within a

21. Harris (1998).

five-pointed star. Many objects we have not encountered before: pillars, some with different sorts of globes atop them. The coffin is particularly noteworthy. We see a ladder; a trowel; a mallet; what appears to be a tic-tac-toe board; on pedestals, two human figures (one of whom holds an anchor, the other, two crossed keys); a beehive; the sun; the moon; seven stars; and the All-Seeing Eye. And is that Noah's ark? And something that looks like a diagram of the Pythagorean theorem?

Are all of these Masonic symbols? Sure, and more that I have not mentioned, as well. For that matter, many Blue Lodge symbols are neither on the apron nor anywhere earlier in this chapter. The Blue Lodge of Freemasonry has many symbols indeed. As we have seen, many of these involve moral lessons about character and conduct; many of these carry multiple layers of symbolism as well. In the so-called high degrees of Freemasonry, like those found in the York and Scottish Rites, there are other symbols that address these themes and introduce the Mason to further esoteric areas of knowledge.[22]

My point here is that Freemasonry is replete with sym-

---

22. I consider the more esoteric symbolism of the Blue Lodge and high degrees in detail in my forthcoming book, tentatively titled *The Esoteric Mysteries of Freemasonry: What the Mysteries of Masonry Mean for You and Your Life.*

bolism that requires reflection and experience to unfold. Over time and with repeated exposure to this symbolism, the character of a Mason deepens and becomes more mature. This is one of the ways in which Freemasonry helps a man to broaden his horizons.

SUMMARY

Some of the symbols of Freemasonry are obvious, some more subtle. Among the more obvious symbols of Blue Lodge Freemasonry, there are the square, the level, the plumb, the compass, the square and compasses together, the altar, the Volume of Sacred Law, the lodge room itself (standing in for parts of the temple built by Solomon), and the letter G. Some of these symbols derive from the tools of the medieval stonemason's trade; many of these symbols have more than one level of interpretation. There are many more symbols in the Blue Lodge, let alone in the high degrees of Freemasonry. The point of this symbolism is to deepen a Mason's character and give him a broader perspective on his life and his place in the universe.

5.

How Freemasonry Began

It is natural to want to know how Freemasonry arose. However, Masonic history is a controversial subject. Much has been written on the subject that is either of a sensationalistic nature, or just plain poor history. On the other hand, there are all sorts of intriguing hints, and unanswered questions, regarding Masonic history.

Here I will address the question of Masonic origins from the perspective of several different periods: (1) the initiatic tradition in ancient times; (2) the medieval Knights Templar; (3) the medieval stonemasons of Europe; (4) the European Enlightenment; and (5) the founding of the first Grand Lodge. In addition, I will describe the role of Freemasonry in the founding of the United States of America.

THE INITIATIC TRADITION IN ANCIENT TIMES

As I mentioned earlier, traditions of initiation were common in many ancient societies. There are indications that initiation occurred in dynastic Egypt, as it certainly did later, in Ptolemaic Egypt, as well as in the ancient Greek mystery schools and in the mystery cult of Mithras that was so important in the Roman Empire. Initiation seems to have been practiced in the Qumran community of ancient Palestine, perhaps among the Merkavah and Hekhalot mystics of the Jewish communities in Babylon and Palestine, and among the early Christian Gnostics.

In addition to full-scale initiation, ancient literature indicates that there were traditions in ancient times about the transmission of secret knowledge. Some of these traditions involve prominent biblical figures, including Adam,[23] Seth,[24] Enoch,[25] and Abraham.[26]

---

23. The kabbalistic text known as the Zohar taught that Adam received powerful esoteric knowledge in a book from the angel Raziel (Zohar 1:55b, 1:37b); portions of the Zohar are available in many translations, including Matt (2004). A book attributed to Raziel has circulated for centuries (Savedow, 2000).

24. The ancient Christian Gnostics taught that Adam received secret revelation that he communicated to his son Seth; see "The Revelation of Adam" in Meyer (2007); see there also the section on Sethian literature (Turner, 2007). See also Zohar 1:55b, 1:72b.

25. Zohar 1:37b, 1:55b, 1:72b. See also the apocryphal books, 1 Enoch (Charles, 2003; Laurence, 2001) and 2 Enoch (Barnstone, 2005).

26. Tvedtnes, Hauglid, and Gee (2001).

What does all this have to do with Masonry today? Some Masonic historians of the eighteenth and early nineteenth century thought that there was a direct connection between the ancient biblical patriarchs and Freemasonry—essentially, they believed that Adam and his righteous descendants were Freemasons. This view is certainly naïve when taken in a literal sense. However, when taken more in a figurative sense, there is something worth considering here.

Human societies have had a concern with initiation for a long, long time. What we see with the emergence of Freemasonry is not exactly an invention of an initiatory tradition from scratch, but rather a re-emergence of initiation as a human concern after a long period when this concern was ignored or even suppressed in Europe.

Let us call the early Masons more concerned with symbols than building cathedrals the first Freemasons. When these first Freemasons formed their first lodges—whenever that was—they did so in the context of human societies having many centuries of tradition about initiation and the transmission of special knowledge. To what extent the early Freemasons were consciously aware of this tradition, we do not now know; however, what we do know, in the light of recorded history, is that the early Freemasons were not developing something entirely new. This opens the possibility that Freemasonry was *inspired*, to some extent, by the ancient initiatic traditions, even if it was not directly descended from them.[27]

THE MEDIEVAL KNIGHTS TEMPLAR

Much has been written about the medieval Knights Templar and the origin of Freemasonry. This is a controversial issue; although I can address it here only briefly, it is a fascinating mystery of Masonic history.

To truly understand the Knights Templar—if that were even possible—would require a thorough understanding of several issues that go beyond our scope here.[28] These would include the life of Christian faith in medieval Europe; medieval Jewish culture; political and religious factors behind the Crusades, which were undertaken to put the Holy Land of Palestine under Christian rule[29]; and the complex Muslim civilization of the time.

For now, it must suffice to say that the Order of the Poor

---

27. I address this possibility at length in Koltko-Rivera (2007).
28. Accounts of the Templars for a popular audience include those written by Hodge (2007), Howarth (1993), Read (1999), and Robinson (1991). Solid histories have been written by Barber (1994) and Partner (1990).
29. Tyerman (2005) provides a good brief overview of the Crusades. Two mutually contrary perspectives on the Crusades are given by Armstrong (2001) and Stark (2009).

Knights of the Temple of Solomon, or the Order of the Temple, was founded in Jerusalem in AD 1118, a generation or so after the First Crusade (AD 1095–1099). The order had the stated purpose of protecting Christian pilgrims in the Holy Land. Better known as the Knights Templar, they were the first group of their type: religious monks who were also warriors, including knights mounted on war horses. They required initiates to offer all their earthly possessions to the order, which thereby became quite wealthy; the order lent some of this wealth (at interest) to kings, thereby becoming *fabulously* wealthy. Being concerned with facilitating travel to the Holy Land, the order implemented a system of international banking, the first of its kind on so large a scale.

The Knights Templar were the most disciplined military force of their time, legendary for their prowess in battle. Although the order ultimately lost the Holy Land despite its best efforts, it endured as a major force in Europe—until destroyed by the treachery of its own allies.

King Philip IV of France coveted the Templars' wealth and forced Pope Clement V to assist him in a plan to obtain it. On Friday, October 13, 1307, Philip arrested every Knight Templar who could be found in France, and over the next several years his agents tortured many of the Templars into confessing to the most grotesque charges of heresy and

blasphemy. The charges were made remotely plausible in
some people's eyes by the long-standing Templar custom of
secrecy, including secret initiations. The pope disbanded
the order in 1312, and Jacques de Molay, the last Grand
Master of the Knights Templar, was burned alive at the stake
near Paris on March 18, 1314. (No doubt it was cold com-
fort to the shades of the knights that in October 2007 the
Vatican Secret Archives published the *Processus Contra
Templarios*, or "Proceedings Against the Templars," including the long-lost Chinon Parchment, which contained Pope
Clement V's absolution of the Templars on the charges of
heresy.[30])

This much is universally accepted history. However,
there is much yet unknown about the Templars. Thousands
of knights escaped arrest, many because they lived in countries that took a relaxed attitude to the pope's orders that
the Templars be arrested. Where did they go?

Over four hundred years after the death of Jacques de
Molay, and twenty years after the formation of the first
Grand Lodge of Freemasons in England (which I describe
later), the teacher and historian Andrew Michael Ramsay,

---

30. The Chancellor Robert R Livingston Masonic Library of Grand Lodge, in
New York City, possesses one of the few copies of the *Processus* that exist in
the United States. A news account of the *Processus* and the Chinon Parchment is given in "Scrap of Parchment," 2007/2008.

a Freemason, composed two versions of an oration for de-
livery at Masonic lodges in France in 1736 and 1737.[31] In his
famous orations, Ramsay claimed that Masonry was trace-
able to knights of the Crusades who later settled in the British Isles. (He did not specifically name the Knights Templar.)

Ramsay gave no evidence for this claim, but from about
that time there has been the impression that the Knights
Templar survived in some fashion after their official destruction, with some of the survivors taking refuge in Scotland and forming the basis for Freemasonry. (It is still
unclear where Ramsay got this idea and whether his orations were its sole source.) This connection to the Templars
became part of the official history of some groups existing on the periphery of Freemasonry, such as the Rite of
Strict Observance, formed just a few years after Ramsay's
orations.[32]

Could any of this be true? In our day, the amateur historian John J. Robinson—not a Freemason at the time—
published a very popular book on the relationship of the
Knights Templar to Freemasonry, *Born in Blood.* In part
of the book, he analyzed various aspects of Masonic ritual

31. Ramsay's orations are given in full by Batham (1992) and analyzed by
Kahler (1992).
32. Bernheim and de Hoyos (2006).

and concluded that the distinctive vocabulary and rituals of Freemasonry show the signs of having been devised by a group of French-speaking knights on the run for their lives—knights just like the Templars.

We may never know whether the fugitive Knights Templar had anything to do with the origins of Freemasonry. What we do know is that the fall of the Templars was a seismic shock to medieval Europe, and the memory of that shock lasted a very long time. (As the story goes, nearly five centuries after the destruction of the Templars, during the French Revolution, just after King Louis XVI had been guillotined in 1793, some anonymous citizen jumped to the platform of execution, dipped his fingers into the king's blood, and proclaimed to the crowd, "Jacques de Molay— *you are avenged!*")

The founders of Freemasonry—whoever they were— were certainly *aware* of the history of the Templars, and they were clearly *inspired* by Templar ideals: devotion to God, a focus on the temple in Jerusalem, dedication and discipline. These founders also remembered the lessons of Templar history: the dangers of both absolute monarchy and the union of church and state.

The Knights Templar are remembered well in Masonry today. The third division of the York Rite is called the Knights Templar, and the medieval knights are prominently featured in the rituals of that division. The medieval Knights Templar are overtly mentioned in some of the degrees of the Scottish Rite. A prominent Masonic organization for young men is DeMolay International. The legend of the last of the Templar Grand Masters appears here and there in various Masonic ceremonies.

Whether the Templars actually laid the foundation for Freemasonry, I cannot say. However, the Templars certainly have been a worthy inspiration to the fraternity for at least three centuries.

THE MEDIEVAL STONEMASONS
OF EUROPE

The very name *Freemason* shows a connection between the fraternity and the stonemason's trade. As we shall see, even this connection is not without controversy.

From antiquity, stonemasons were practitioners of a very special trade. Those who directed stonemasons needed knowledge in geometry and mathematics, knowledge held by few in medieval times. In addition, they required a knowledge of legend, scripture, and art to devise the more decorative aspects of their structures.

By the nature of their work, stonemasons had unusual

privileges that were highly valued in medieval times: they were permitted to change location and residence freely. Stonemasons' careers might take them across hundreds of miles. The work on a cathedral, say, might mean that stonemasons from a great distance, many of whom had never met one another, might work on a project together. (This was entirely different from, say, the cobblers' guild in a given town, where each member knew all the other members throughout their entire working careers. Most people other than stonemasons were prohibited by law from moving from place to place.) "All this meant that the needs of the mason in terms of organization and relations with his fellows were rather different from those of most other craftsmen."[33]

To protect their trade, stonemasons preserved much of their practical knowledge as a set of trade secrets. In an era without union cards, those privileged to know these secrets were formally invested with a set of secret signs of recognition, such as handgrips and words, which identified them as legitimate practitioners of the stonemason trade.

Masonic historians have long traced Freemasons' customs of signs of recognition and the possession of special

---

33. Stevenson (1988), p. 13, spelling Americanized.

knowledge through the history of the medieval stonemasons.[34] It appears to be the case that by the late sixteenth century stonemason lodges in Britain faced a crisis that may have led to the formation of modern Masonry.

Gothic architecture was on the decline in this era; business left the stonemasons in favor of the bricklayers, who needed less skill and fewer trade secrets than the stonemasons to ply their trade. The rediscovery of Euclid's geometry during the Renaissance meant that many of the stonemasons' trade secrets became public knowledge; thus, men who were not initiated members of stonemason lodges could apply knowledge of geometry to carry out some of the stonemasons' activities in erecting a building. The stonemason lodges found themselves in a precarious position, with declining membership.

In this situation, or so the story goes, the stonemason lodges made membership available to gentlemen who did not actually work with stone; these men were "accepted" as masons, even though they were not craftsmen; thus, they

---

34. A classic reference for this viewpoint is Knoop and Jones (1978). Concerning Italian stonemasons, see Ravenscroft (1946). A possible connection between the Knights Templar and medieval stonemasons is explored at length by Naudon (2005).

were "nonoperative" masons. The best available documentation indicates that this first happened in Scotland, around 1590.[35] This process spread to England. The noted scholar Elias Ashmole became a Freemason in 1646, leaving in his diary the first record that we have of someone becoming a Mason in an English lodge; however, it has been ascertained that everyone he mentioned in his diary as a lodge member was nonoperative, so clearly Ashmole was not the first English gentleman made an accepted Freemason, probably by a wide margin.

Of course, this raises all sorts of questions. In as class-conscious a society as England was (with Scotland not far behind, if at all, in that department), what were land-owning gentlemen and educated scholars doing becoming members of stonemasons' lodges—basically a sort of trade union or craft guild? This just seems very out of character for the gentlemen and scholars involved. To answer this question, we must consider the intellectual climate of the late sixteenth through early eighteenth centuries.

---

35. Stevenson (1988, 2001).

THE LATE RENAISSANCE AND
EARLY ENLIGHTENMENT

The collapse of the western part of the Roman Empire in the fifth century AD saw the disappearance of much of the scientific, philosophical, and speculative literature of the ancient world from the knowledge of Europe. Libraries were burned, manuscripts destroyed, and learned people killed as the invaders sacked Rome and its outposts.

It was not until the Renaissance (roughly the fourteenth through seventeenth centuries) that knowledge of classical arts and sciences was reborn in European society. This period also saw a rebirth of interest in the symbol systems and esoteric knowledge of the ancients, including Hermetic philosophy, alchemy, and astrology. A major Renaissance theme was the belief that the universe could be understood and mastered by a "science" that was not strongly differentiated from magic. Studies in alchemy, astrology, and esoteric practices were important to many scholars of the day.[36] In addition, in the 1640s, many European schol-

---

36. This situation is described at length by Yates (1991). See also Stevenson (1988) and MacNulty (1991, pp. 11–15).

ars were concerned with the appearance of the Rosicrucian manifestos, which told of a secret brotherhood of alchemical healers.[37]

Scholarly preoccupation with such esoteric studies as alchemical and magical symbolism continued throughout the Renaissance and deep into the Enlightenment. Although the Enlightenment is usually thought of as a period where reason was applied as a way to control nature, the foundation of the Enlightenment was deeply positioned in the attempt to control nature by the esoteric wisdom of the ancients—including the symbolic wisdom of, for example, alchemy.[38] Elias Ashmole, the scholar mentioned above as an early English Freemason, was deeply interested in alchemy and attempted to make known to the purportedly hidden Rosicrucian brotherhood his desire to join them; he was joined in this desire by many scholars of his era.[39] Isaac Newton himself, the most brilliant scientist of his era (indeed, perhaps any era), is estimated to have written more

---

37. The Rosicrucians (McIntosh, 1998) may never have existed as anything but an idea, but this idea had far-reaching consequences (Yates, 1972). The concern of early Freemasons with Rosicrucianism is addressed by Millar (2005); see his Chapter 3.

38. The conventional approach to the Enlightenment is illustrated in the readings chosen by Kramnick (1995). The esoteric roots of the Enlightenment are considered at length by Yates (1972).

39. Churton (2002, 2006).

about esoteric religion and alchemy than he did about what we now consider conventional science.[40]

These interests—particularly the interest in hermetic or alchemical symbolism—may have led some of the learned gentlemen of Scotland and England to enter the stonemasons' lodges. It may be that the stonemasons' ceremonies of initiation were already deeply symbolic, and the learned gentlemen sought the deeper meanings of that symbolism. Alternatively, perhaps the secrecy of the stonemasons' lodges provided a convenient cover for the learned gentlemen to pursue their own explorations of symbolism. One way or the other, it is certain that learned gentlemen entered stonemasons' lodges, and many of these gentlemen were deeply interested in alchemical and esoteric symbolism.

Thus came about a transition from "operative" Masonry—that is, the ritual of people who actually worked with stone—to "speculative," "symbolic," or "philosophical" Masonry—the ritual of people "accepted" as Masons, even though they never worked with stone.

---

40. For Newton's alchemical interests, see White (1997) and Fanning (2009). Although Newton was not a Freemason, many of his scientific colleagues in the Royal Society shared his intellectual interests, and were Freemasons; see Bauer (2007).

THE FOUNDING OF THE FIRST GRAND LODGE

We know relatively little about the activities of the early symbolic lodges. What we do know is that a small group of them is said to have come together at a tavern in London in 1717 and formed the first Grand Lodge. This was an important turning point in Masonic history.

A Grand Lodge is an overarching organization with authority over a group of local lodges. (In the United States, there is a Grand Lodge for each of the states, plus one each for the District of Columbia and Puerto Rico.)

The formation of the first Grand Lodge of England was controversial. Some other lodges in the British Isles felt that the London lodges were asserting authority that they did not have. (It took almost a century to sort out competing claims of priority and authority.)

What is *not* disputed is that the advent of the Grand Lodge form of Freemasonry was a revolutionary development in two ways. First, Freemasonry had become public. Masonic *ceremonies* remained private, but the *existence* of Freemasonry itself became common knowledge.

Secondly, the advent of the Grand Lodge advanced the spread of Freemasonry in unexpected ways. Perhaps because the Grand Lodge took upon itself the authority to charter lodges, there was now a clear authority to turn to when one wished to form a new lodge, say, down the street, or in the community down the road—or in India.

Within a generation or two of the founding of the Grand Lodge, there were Masonic lodges in every colony of England, in almost all of the countries of Europe, and in many of *their* colonies as well. The spread of Freemasonry was explosive and widespread in many places—including the English colonies in North America.[41]

FREEMASONRY AND THE FOUNDING OF THE UNITED STATES

In some quarters, it is held that the American Revolution was some sort of Masonic project. It is easy to think this way, given that such notable Revolutionary figures as George Washington, Paul Revere, and Benjamin Franklin were all Freemasons. However, this ignores the fact that quite a number of British military leaders were Freemasons as well. The fact is, Freemasonry *did* make central contributions to

---

41. For a brief history of the spread of Masonry in the United States, see Van Doren (2004).

the founding of the United States—but not so much in the Revolution as in the Constitution.

Fourteen of the fifty-five delegates to the Constitutional Convention in 1787 (and nine of the thirty-nine signers of the Constitution) were Freemasons, including George Washington and Benjamin Franklin.[42] The values underlying the Constitution show a remarkable resemblance to the values of the Masonic lodge—values which were almost nowhere else to be found in the culture of Europe in that era.

- The Masonic lodge elected its leaders by popular vote. This kind of democracy had hardly been seen since the height of the Roman Republic and, before that, the ancient Greek democracies. Most of 1787 Europe was governed by some form of monarchy. Of course, the U.S. Constitution bases the American government on elections.[43]
- The Masonic lodge allowed men of all religions to become members. This was highly unusual in the Europe of the time, where most governments gave official support to some church, and people of other religions

---

42. See Coil (1996, p. 621); six other delegates became Masons later.
43. U.S. Constitution, Art. II, Sect. 1, amended by Twelfth Amendment.

often suffered various legal consequences, including imprisonment or even execution. Of course, the U.S. Constitution specifically forbids Congress to establish a favored religion and establishes the rights of members of all religions (or no religion) to equal protection under the law.[44]

• Freemasonry put all men on an equal footing in the lodge. Yes, there was a leadership structure—but it rotated, usually annually. This was highly unusual in the Europe of the time, where some people held titles of nobility, often from birth. The U.S. Constitution, on the other hand, specifically forbids Congress to grant titles of nobility (and, presumably, the privileges that come with such titles).[45]

Some scholars have said that the Masonic lodge prepared the citizens of a newly independent America (and the citizens of Europe generally) to be part of a country directed by an elected government, which (ideally) treated all citizens equally under the law and guaranteed them reli-

---

44. U.S. Constitution, Amendment I (Bill of Rights).
45. U.S. Constitution, Article I, Section 9.

gious freedom.[46] It seems to me that the way that the values of the U.S. Constitution resemble the values of the Masonic lodge can hardly be a coincidence.

SUMMARY

Freemasonry resembles in some of its objectives the ancient mystery schools, which focused on individual enlightenment through the initiatory experience. However, there is little or nothing in the way of hard evidence directly connecting Freemasonry to the ancients. Similarly, Freemasonry is inspired by the example of the medieval Knights Templar. Although there is tantalizing suggestive evidence, a direct connection between the Templars and Freemasonry has not been established.

Medieval stonemasons had many distinctive characteristics compared to other artisans. They had specialized knowledge of geometry and secret signs of recognition. Modern Freemasonry borrows a great deal of symbolism from the traditional tools of the medieval stonemasons.

At least some of the early Freemasons appear to have been men interested in the symbolism of alchemy and her-

---

46. Jacob (1991, 2006).

metic esoteric studies, who were drawn for some reason to the symbolic initiations of the stonemason lodges. These gentlemen were "accepted" into the stonemason lodges as "masons," even though these gentlemen never worked in stone. Eventually, they came to dominate the stonemasons' lodges completely.

In 1717, the first Grand Lodge was organized in London, from which Freemasonry spread around the world. Freemasonry may have transmitted some of its values to the American Constitution itself, including the practice of democratic elections, religious tolerance, and egalitarianism.

6.

Masonic Controversies

Like any sizable social organization, Freemasonry has its controversial aspects. In this chapter, I consider several such aspects: Masonry's stance toward women; its stance toward African Americans; an important nineteenth-century Masonic leader, Albert Pike; and proposals in the United Kingdom to require the registration of Freemasons in the justice system, law enforcement, and the military. (I consider anti-Masonic conspiracy theories, another area of controversy, in Chapter 7.)

WOMEN AND FREEMASONRY

Mainstream Freemasonry[47] is an all-male organization. How can one defend the existence of an all-male organization in the twenty-first century? How does this jibe with Masonry's egalitarian ethos? Is the exclusion of women from mainstream Freemasonry a form of sexism? Am I saying that there are no opportunities at all for an initiatory experience for women within Freemasonry? I take three angles of approach to these issues.

FREEMASONRY HAS A RIGHT
TO BE A FRATERNITY

Mainstream Freemasonry has always defined itself as a *fraternity*, that is, as an organization for men. The guiding legends and mythic structure of mainstream Freemasonry

---

47. The question of what is "mainstream Freemasonry" is itself a complex question. For our purposes, I define mainstream Freemasonry as those forms of Freemasonry practiced by Grand Lodges who have been chartered by, and are recognized as "regular" Freemasonry by, the United Grand Lodge of England (UGLE). UGLE has standards such as requiring candidates for Masonry to hold a belief in a Supreme Being, and so forth.

involve the builders of the ancient temple dedicated by King Solomon and medieval groups like the stonemasons of Europe and the Knights Templar; mainstream Freemasonry conforms to the all-male nature of those organizations. Mainstream Freemasonry has no more reason to apologize for being an all-male organization than do the Boy Scouts of America.

One frequently cited basis for criticism about all-male organizations (such as some country clubs or business networking groups) is that they can restrict women from having access to premises where business deals are negotiated, even informally. This is a legitimate issue, to be sure; however, it is not a serious concern for the Masonic lodge, which simply is not a place where one's professional business should be conducted. I have heard brethren actively discourage individuals from submitting petitions (applications) to become Freemasons because those individuals were primarily interested in networking for business purposes. Candidates are required to swear that their interest in Freemasonry is not based on the motive of improving their business or financial position. The exclusion of women from mainstream Freemasonry has at most a minimal effect on women in business.

THERE ARE MASONIC-AFFILIATED
ORGANIZATIONS THAT INVOLVE WOMEN

Although mainstream *Freemasonry* itself is an all-male organization, there are other organizations, *affiliated with
but independent from* Freemasonry, that do admit women,
sometimes exclusively. These are not "ladies' auxiliary"
organizations in the usual sense of that term. These organizations manage themselves and typically confer degrees or
ceremonies of initiation on their members. They include
the following.

The Order of the Eastern Star, the Order of the Amaranth,
and *the White Shrine of Jerusalem.* The Eastern Star is an
organization for both Master Masons and their female relatives (like a spouse, sister, or descendant) who believe in
the existence of a Divine Being. (The Eastern Star in New
York State does not require women to have any Masonic
connection; in New Jersey, members must be Christian.)
The Order of the Amaranth is a similar organization; the
White Shrine of Jerusalem is a similar organization open to
Christians.

The Social Order of the Beauceant. This is an all-women's
group (a "ladies' fraternal order," as their website puts it)
for female relatives of Master Masons who have obtained

the Knight Templar degree within the York Rite. (Being affiliated with the Templars, the order is Christian.)

The Heroines of Jericho, Ladies of the Circle of Perfection, and *the Cyrene Crusaders.* These are all-women's groups for female relatives of York Rite Masons of the Prince Hall Affiliation (see page 100). Respectively, these are for female relatives of Royal Arch Masons, Royal and Select Masters, and Knights Templar, within the York Rite.

The Ladies of the Oriental Shrine, the Daughters of the Nile, and *the Daughters of Isis.* These are all-women's groups for female relatives of Master Masons who are also members of the Shriners. The Daughters of the Nile is associated with the Prince Hall Affiliation (see below).

Order of the Golden Circle. This is an all-women's group for female relatives of Prince Hall Scottish Rite Masons.

Job's Daughters International and *the International Order of Rainbow for Girls.* These are youth groups for girls and young women. Job's Daughters is open to relatives of Freemasons; the Rainbow no longer requires a Masonic relative.

Thus, there are initiatory experiences with a mainstream Masonic heritage that are open to women of all ages. Although these groups usually have an affiliation with a Masonic lodge, the adult groups, at the least, are administratively independent and are run by their own members.

ALTERNATIVE FORMS OF FREEMASONRY INVOLVE WOMEN, AS WELL

There are alternative forms of Freemasonry outside of the mainstream that have admitted women for well over a century. Masonic lodges for men and women are known by such names as Co-Masonry and *Le Droit Humain* (French for "human rights").

Entire Grand Lodge organizations exist for all-female lodges, such as the Grand Loge Féminine de France and the Women's Grand Lodge of Belgium, which have chartered women's lodges in the United States and Canada. The Order of Women Freemasons reportedly includes three hundred lodges, primarily in England.

AFRICAN AMERICANS AND FREEMASONRY

The history that Freemasonry has with African Americans is complex and tortured, and frankly does not speak well of Freemasonry as it has been practiced in certain eras and places. There are really two issues to consider with reference to Freemasonry and African Americans: the reception of African Americans into regular Masonic lodges, and the recognition by the Masonic mainstream of lodges that are part of what is called the Prince Hall Affiliation and organizations like it.

THE RECEPTION OF AFRICAN AMERICANS INTO MASONIC LODGES

Like many American institutions in the eighteenth through the early twentieth centuries, Freemasonry at large once discriminated against African Americans in terms of admission as Master Masons. This was racism, pure and simple.

The exclusion of African Americans was entirely different from the exclusion of women from Freemasonry. There was nothing in the foundational legends or mythos of Freemasonry that justified exclusion of African Americans. Masonry does require that its candidates not be slaves, but this does not justify the exclusion of free African Americans. The exclusion of African Americans from the historically White lodges of the Colonial period and thereafter was a blot on the fraternal reputation of Freemasonry, which aspired to promote the ideals of universal brotherhood.

We might call the Masonic mainstream the "Free and Accepted Masons" or F&AM lodges. After centuries of racial exclusiveness, by the late twentieth century, F&AM Masons in most parts of the United States, like most Americans, had rejected racial criteria (even informally) for admission to Freemasonry. For example, I was made a Master Mason as one of a group of three candidates, at Winter Park Lodge #239 F&AM, in Florida (near Orlando). One of my brother candidates that day was a dark-skinned African American. After moving back to New York City in 2008, I found that African American Masons were evident in every Masonic body that I visited, many in prominent leadership positions.

This does not mean that racism is extinct from Freemasonry. In 2009, in the Grand Lodge of one state of the American South, the Masonic initiation of an African American was such an exceedingly rare event, and the furor that this initiation created among some Southern Masons was so great, that it made the pages of *The New York Times*.[48] It is hard to escape the impression that there were many members of this Grand Lodge who held what can only be described as racist attitudes. However, I expect that the rising of a new generation of Masons who are more progressive than some of their elders will doubtless change this picture within, I hope, a few years.

Nonetheless, this is only half the story.

---

48. Dewan and Brown (2009).

THE RECOGNITION
OF PRINCE HALL LODGES

In 1775, the year before the formal beginning of the
American War of Independence or Revolutionary War, a
traveling British Military lodge (Irish Constitution Military Lodge No. 441) initiated over a dozen African American men (likely freeborn) in Massachusetts, including an
individual named Prince Hall. After the British military
unit left the area three weeks later, taking their lodge
with them, these African American Masons functioned
as a Masonic lodge; they received a charter from the
Grand Lodge of England in 1784 and formed African Lodge
#459. After they (like all American lodges) were stricken
from the rolls of the United Grand Lodge of England in
1813, African Lodge ultimately declared itself independent of English Freemasonry in 1827, as many F&AM
lodges already had. African Lodge was not permitted to
affiliate their lodge with any of the existing F&AM Grand
Lodges (all essentially composed of White Masons) in the
former colonies. These African American Masons pro-
ceeded to charter other lodges in what has become known
as the Prince Hall style of Freemasonry, prominent
today in such organizations as the Prince Hall Affilia-

tion.[49] Prince Hall Affiliation, or PHA, lodges have a well-deserved reputation for honor, and precision in their Masonic work; they have long been noted for their contributions to their communities.

For many years, the F&AM Masonic lodges cried foul and would not recognize the Prince Hall lodges as legitimately Masonic. However, in the late twentieth century especially, a number of leading American Masonic thinkers began to realize that this situation was manifestly unfair, and that the denial of recognition of the Prince Hall lodges as legitimately Masonic was a disguised form of racism. The movement for Masonic recognition of the Prince Hall lodges as legitimate picked up steam in the 1980s and 1990s. As I write this (in mid-2010), all but ten of the fifty-two F&AM Grand Lodges in the United States have recognized a Prince Hall Grand Lodge in their state as legitimate; in many of these jurisdictions, mutual visitation is possible, so brethren from a Prince Hall lodge can attend an F&AM lodge and vice versa.

The ten U.S. F&AM Grand Lodges that do not recognize any Prince Hall Grand Lodge as legitimate are all in the

---

49. See Roundtree and Bessel (2006). See also Coil (1996) under entry for "Black Freemasonry," pp. 98–102.

American southeast, the heartland of the old Confederacy. I do not think that this is accidental. However, here too, I expect that the rising generation of Freemasons will be dominated with those who are liberated from the regressive racial attitudes of their forefathers.

African American men interested in Freemasonry would do well to consider either the F&AM lodges or the Prince Hall lodges. Such gentlemen would certainly be welcome in any lodge that I have ever visited.

ALBERT PIKE

The next area of controversy that I shall consider here involves one of the most famous Freemasons in all of American history: Albert Pike (1809–1891). Brother Pike is not controversial for his *actual* Masonic activities, but for his *purported* activities, and for his status as a former general of the Confederate Army during the American Civil War.

There are some damning allegations made against Pike: that he helped the Knights of the Golden Circle, an organization that provided help to the Confederacy during and, allegedly, even after the Civil War; that he was involved in the formation of the Ku Klux Klan after the war; even that he was a Satanist. Each of these allegations—widely available on the Internet and elsewhere—casts a shadow not only on Pike, but on the Masonic organizations of which he was a part. I shall consider each of these charges in turn.

It is important to respond to allegations like these. In his day, Albert Pike led at one time or another almost all of the important Masonic organizations. The most spectacular example of his leadership involves the organization where he is best remembered, the Scottish Rite in the Southern Jurisdiction,[50] whose rituals he thoroughly revised and whose membership—along with that of Freemasonry in general—Pike vastly increased. Pike wrote some of the most penetrating analyses ever printed regarding Masonic symbolism.[51] In addition, his Scottish Rite rituals have exposed countless Freemasons to a variety of religious and spiritual philosophies that they otherwise might never have encountered.[52] Yet, perhaps because of his many contribu-

---

50. The Supreme Council, 33° of the Southern Jurisdiction in the United States of America—the first Scottish Rite Supreme Council in the world—covers the thirty-five states that are south of the Mason-Dixon Line or west of the Mississippi, as well as the District of Columbia. The Northern Masonic Jurisdiction covers the other fifteen states in the Northeast and northern Midwest.
51. For example, de Hoyos (2008).
52. See Hutchens (1995, 2006).

tions to Freemasonry, Pike is something of a lightning rod for anti-Masonic accusations to this day. In a way, an attack on Pike is an expression of an attack on Masonry; that is why I consider these allegations here.

PIKE AND THE KNIGHTS OF THE GOLDEN CIRCLE

The Knights of the Golden Circle (KGC) was an organization that sought to promote the interests of the American South in the years preceding the Civil War. Once the war broke out, the KGC functioned as something of a "fifth column" organization, publicly seeking to undercut support for the war and secretly providing support to the Confederacy.[53]

The KGC seemed to disappear at the end of the war. However, it has been alleged that the KGC continued its activities in secret after the war, both hiding and protecting the legendary hoard of gold that the Confederacy had accumulated for the day when the South should rise again.

Such stories have circulated for many years; I take no position here on the plausibility of those ideas. What concerns me here are the stories that some circulate to the effect that

---

53. The verifiable history of the KGC is told in several sources: Crenshaw (1941), Dunn (1967), Hicks (1961), R. E. May (1973).

the KGC recruited Albert Pike—then the head of the Scottish Rite in the Southern Jurisdiction—to help them in the task of transporting and protecting the Confederate gold.

Two authors in particular have made the case that the sophisticated organization of the Scottish Rite would have been very useful to the KGC in carrying out their mission. They state that their depiction of events is "based on what is largely circumstantial evidence that plausibly links key players, places and organizations in a convincing, interpretive framework."[54]

Although these authors have done interesting field research regarding the possible survival of the KGC after the Civil War, their research regarding Albert Pike is far more problematic. The "evidence," such as it is, is essentially composed of the fact that it would have been very convenient indeed for the KGC if the organization and resources of the Scottish Rite had been placed at the service of the KGC. However, the authors' book provides no actual evidence—no memorandum, no diary entry, no direct per-

---

54. Getler and Brewer (2003), p. 43. More recently, the first author of that book stated that "research I have been involved with over the last decade suggests that the KGC had direct ties to the Scottish Rite's Southern Jurisdiction, led by Pike during and after the Civil War" (Getler, 2009, p. 73); however, he produces no evidence of such "direct ties," leading me to believe that he has nothing to add to the conjectures that he advanced in his 2003 book.

sonal testimony—suggesting that the Scottish Rite actually *was* placed at the service of the KGC. The case is based entirely on supposition. In sum, there is no tangible evidence that Albert Pike had anything at all to do with the Knights of the Golden Circle.

PIKE AND THE KU KLUX KLAN

It is widely reported on the Internet that Albert Pike was somehow involved in the Ku Klux Klan. The author of the definitive biography on Pike had the following to say about this notion:

> I have found no contemporary, nor no reliable late evidence that Pike ever joined the Klan. Yet in at least three unreliable histories of the Klan, it is stated that he was either attorney general or a high-ranking official of the order. Allen W. Trelease, the most recent and most authoritative historian of the Klan casts doubt on Pike's membership. The Prescript, or constitution, of the order provides for no such officer, he says.[55]

55. Brown (1997), p. 439, footnotes omitted. The three Klan histories that Brown described as "unreliable" were all first published between 1905 and 1924; Pike had died in 1891, and so was not able to respond personally to these allegations.

No doubt the Klan would have liked to recruit Pike's name to their cause because of the great respect in which his name was held, as the longtime leader of the Scottish Rite in the South. However, here again, the fact that Pike's affiliation *would* have helped the Klan's cause is no proof at all that Pike actually *was* so affiliated. The hard fact of the matter is that, here again, there is no actual evidence— no memorandum, no personal eyewitness—to support this allegation.

It is true that, in an editorial of April 16, 1868, Pike stated that the rights of White citizens in the chaotic South of the Reconstruction era would best be protected by a "secret association" of some sort. However, in this editorial, Pike specifically disqualified the Klan of his day for that role. Pike stated that members would be in such a secret association, "not . . . to commit follies and outrages; but for mutual, peaceful, lawful, self-defence."[56] Given the well-documented offenses committed against the citizens of the South during Reconstruction, one can understand why Pike would desire such a vehicle to protect his community; given the well-documented "follies and outrages" committed by the Klan, it is clear that Pike was not looking to the KKK to fit the role of his "secret association." Of course, Pike had a

56. Brown (1997), p. 439.

very long association with Freemasonry, the praises of which he had often sung. In that context, it seems likely that Pike's hope, expressed in this editorial, was that *Freemasonry* would be the "secret association" to step into the power vacuum of the Reconstruction and provide for the common welfare. This was, perhaps, a romantic notion, but Pike was a larger-than-life figure, full of grand notions; such a concept would have been nothing unusual for him to produce.

In sum, there is no actual direct evidence that Pike ever had anything to do with the Klan, other than to criticize it. All claims to the contrary are but wishful thinking.

PIKE AND SATANISM

Plug the phrase "yes, Lucifer is God" (with the quotation marks) into your favorite Internet search engine. My Google search on August 17, 2010, returned about 114,000 links; having checked a couple of dozen of these, my guess is that, by far, most of these links attribute the phrase to Albert Pike. The phrase is part of the following passage, attributed to Pike, who supposedly said this in a conference of thirty-third-degree (33°) Scottish Rite Masons:

To you, Sovereign Grand Inspectors General, we say this, that you may repeat it to the Brethren of the 32nd, 31st, and 30th degrees—The Masonic Religion should be, by all of us initiates of the high degrees, maintained in the purity of the Luciferian Doctrine. . . .

Yes, Lucifer is God, and unfortunately Adonay[57] is also god. For the eternal law is that there is no light without shade, . . . for the absolute can only exist as two gods: darkness being necessary for light to serve as its foil as the pedestal is necessary to the statue, and the brake to the locomotive.

Thus, the doctrine of Satanism is a heresy; and the true and pure philosophical religion is the belief in Lucifer, the equal of Adonay; but Lucifer, God of Light and God of Good, is struggling for humanity against Adonay, the God of Darkness and Evil. (Instructions to the 23 Supreme Councils of the World, Albert Pike, Grand Commander, Sovereign Pontiff of Universal Freemasonry, July 14, 1889. Recorded by A. C. De La Rive, *La Femme et l'Enfant dans la Franc-Maçonnerie Universelle*, page 588.)[58]

---

57. That is, *Adonai*, Hebrew for "Lord," one of the names or titles of the Supreme Being used in the Hebrew Bible.
58. The quote is widely available on the Internet and in anti-Masonic literature. I retrieved this text on February 9, 2010, from http://www.biblebelievers.org.au/mason1.htm. It is also available in de Hoyos and Morris (2004), pp. 37–38.

This is not just a hot item; it is downright radioactive. It positions Pike at the center of a revival of an ancient Christian heresy, a Gnostic- or Manichaean-style dualism such as the world had not seen for over a thousand years. And he comes out in favor of the *devil's* side of the equation!

Just one little thing, though. This passage is a complete fabrication.

This passage apparently was created by notorious French anti-Mason Léo Taxil, sometime between 1891 and 1894. It was published by Abel Clarin de la Rive in a book whose French title, translated into English, is *Woman and Child in Universal Freemasonry*, in 1894—conveniently, three years following Pike's death. At a press conference in Paris in 1897, Taxil confessed that he had made up everything he had ever published about devil worship in Freemasonry as part of an immense hoax spanning over a decade. Immediately, de la Rive recanted what he had heard from Taxil, in disgust.

However, the quote was picked up by Lady Queenborough, Edith Starr Miller, who reprinted it in her influential English work, *Occult Theocrasy*, in 1933—apparently unaware that it was the product of a hoax. From Edith Starr Miller, the quote has been picked up by many anti-Masons around the world.[59]

---

59. Taxil's hoax is described in detail by de Hoyos and Morris (2004,

As evidenced by his publications and private letters, Albert Pike "was, in fact, a Christian, who frequently urged his fellows to follow the teachings and example of Jesus of Nazareth."[60] He certainly had nothing to do with Satanism or Luciferianism.

VIOLATING MASONIC CIVIL RIGHTS IN ENGLAND

The first Grand Lodge of Freemasonry was founded in London in 1717. With such a history, one might expect that Freemasonry would enjoy particular respect in England. Sadly, not only is this not so, but recent years have seen shocking governmental actions that would violate the civil rights of Freemasons in England. The inspiration for this turn of events was the 1984 publication of Stephen Knight's book, *The Brotherhood: The Secret World of the*

Chapter 2), who reproduce Taxil's public confession (Bernheim et al., 1996) in an appendix. The website of the Grand Lodge of British Columbia and Yukon also addresses aspects of this scandal: "Abel Claren de la Rive" (2001), "A Hoax" (2001), "Léo Taxil's Confession" (2001), "The Lie of Luciferianism" (2002), and "Occult Theocrasy Notes" (2007).

60. Arturo de Hoyos, in his note (p. 299) introducing selections from Pike's writings illustrating Pike's Christian faith: de Hoyos (2008), Appendix Four, pp. 299–308.

Freemasons.[61] In *The Brotherhood*, Knight wove a tale of police corruption and other criminal doings involving Freemasons based on a string of innuendo, unsubstantiated rumor, and misrepresentations of Masonry. The overall effect was to portray Masonry as a dangerous criminal enterprise, even as Knight exhibited a profound lack of understanding of much of Freemasonry.

One example of this lack of understanding was Knight's description of the infamous Propaganda Due, or P2, lodge in Italy. The P2 lodge was involved with organized crime and money laundering on a monumental scale, some of the facts of which became publicly known in 1981, in revelations that brought down the Italian government. In *The Brotherhood*, Knight discussed the scandal in some detail, but neglected to mention a crucial point: the Grand Lodge of Italy had closed the P2 lodge in 1976, stripping it of its Masonic charter and expelling its master from Masonry altogether.[62] In essence, P2 committed its crimes as a renegade lodge, broken off from legitimate Freemasonry. Here, as in many places, *The Brotherhood* missed crucial issues, thereby

---

61. Knight (1984/1986). We will meet Knight and his anti-Masonic accusations again in Chapter 8, during our discussion of his book on Jack the Ripper (Knight, 1976/1982).
62. "P2 Lodge" (2010).

painting an extremely sinister but highly inaccurate picture of Freemasonry.

However, its many faults notwithstanding, *The Brotherhood* was a bestseller in England, and it affected public opinion mightily. By the end of the decade, suspicions similar to those raised by *The Brotherhood* were used by a particularly ambitious member of Parliament to encourage local civil governments in England to ask job applicants whether they had ever been Freemasons.[63]

This ultimately led to national action. Beginning in 1995, the Home Affairs Select Committee of the House of Commons (roughly equivalent to an American Congressional committee) conducted a two-year investigation of the influence of Freemasonry on police officers and judges. Their report,[64] issued in March 1997, declared that there was nothing sinister about Freemasonry itself, and that there was little if any evidence of "masonic corruption" in the police force or judiciary. However, due to political pressure,[65] the report was amended so as to recommend that police officers, judges, and others be required to register membership

---

63. Hamill (2000/2002).
64. "Freemasonry in the Police and the Judiciary" (1997).
65. Hamill (1997).

in any so-called secret society—a recommendation that made no sense in light of the actual findings of the report itself.[66] Subsequent to the report, England began to require members of the judiciary to declare publicly whether they were Masons, or to publicly decline the question.[67]

After another lengthy inquiry, the Home Affairs Committee issued another report[68] regarding Freemasonry in public life in general. This report reached a number of interestingly worded conclusions. For example, in regard to the troubled West Midlands Serious Crime Squad, the report concluded, "freemasonry was not a primary cause of the difficulties within the Serious Crimes Squad although we cannot entirely exclude the possibility that it may have been a contributory factor." Similarly, in relation to the bad police policies allegedly promulgated by Assistant Chief Constable Stalker of Manchester, the report stated that "we cannot conclude that freemasonry played a significant part in the Stalker affair. We cannot, however, entirely exclude the possibility that it did." Of course, each of these statements is

---

66. The Spring 1998 issue of *Freemasonry Today* has several articles on the Home Office report on Freemasonry in the police and the judiciary; see http://www.freemasonrytoday.com/public/index-04.php
67. "Government Registry of Judiciary Masons" (1998), "Home Office to Pursue Register" (2000).
68. "Freemasonry in Public Life" (1999). Cp. "Grand Lodge Responds" (1999).

logically equivalent to saying, "we have no real evidence that Mary murdered John, although we cannot entirely rule out that possibility." And how often can one *entirely* rule out a possibility? The net effect of such statements was to spread innuendo and needless suspicion, in contradiction to the actual facts discovered.

Of course, all subtleties were lost on some newspaper editors. To one paper, the report's inability to rule out Masonic involvement in the Stalker affair translated to Masonic guilt: as the headline put it, the Select Committee stated that Masons "had role in Stalker case."[69]

Perhaps in keeping with these distorted perceptions, the British Ministry of Defence planned a register of Freemasons in the military.[70] (These plans were abandoned after Masons appealed to the High Court.[71])

English Freemasons were appalled at these events. Masons were being told that registration measures were to be taken because there was "a public perception" of corruption, even though there was no real evidence of corruption; Masons responded that innuendo and groundless perceptions should not drive legislation, and that mandatory

---

69. Waugh (1999).

70. "Judicial Review Warning" (2000).

71. "MoD 'withdraws' its instruction on Masons" (2000/2001).

registration of Freemasons only strengthened the unjustified public perceptions of wrongdoing. Masons pointed out that this was unconscionable discrimination and that mandatory registration smacked of a slippery slope to governmental control of private behavior.

Ultimately, what seems to have made a difference is the European Convention on Human Rights, which became incorporated into English law in October 2000.[72] From 2002 to 2009, the European Court of Human Rights made two significant rulings relevant to these issues.

> First, they ruled that Freemasonry is neither a secret society nor a criminal or illegal organization. Secondly, they have ruled that in a modern democracy it is discriminatory to require anyone accepting public office or public employment to declare whether or not they are Freemasons.[73]

As of this writing, English judges are no longer required nationwide to make a public declaration regarding their Masonic involvement. The issue of the mandatory declaration of Masonry among police officers and others probably will be fought out for years at the level of local government.

---

72. Hamill (2000/2002).
73. "Pro Grand Master Outlines" (2009/2010), p. 7.

There are several lessons to be learned from this controversy. On one level, it is clear that public perception can have vast consequences, no matter how inaccurate these perceptions may be. More specific to Freemasonry, it appears that there is a bubbling pit of anti-Masonic sentiment in the public (un)conscious, just waiting for an opportunity to spill over into public life, with potentially disastrous consequences.

Why might this be so? There are several factors at work here. Although Freemasonry is not a secret society in any real sense—check your phone book under "Fraternal Organizations," and you will find Freemasons pretty easily—Masonry certainly keeps its ceremonies private. Masonic privacy provides an opportunity for people to project their worst fears onto Freemasonry, as quickly as these fears would be projected onto any Rorschach inkblot.[74] In a highly class-conscious society such as that of the United Kingdom,

---

74. This is the looser sense of the term "projection," indicating that people use their individually typical, reflexive ways of responding when confronted with ambiguous situations (Henry, 1956, p. 31); basically, people project their "stuff" onto the page, as it were. In the narrower sense of the term, people project onto others, or onto ambiguous situations, the socially unacceptable aspects of their own personalities (Hammer, 1958, p. 53; Schafer, 1954, p. 279), resulting in "the translation of internally experienced dangers into external dangers" (Exner, 2003, p. 20)—an interesting possibility to consider when it comes to rumors about Freemasons.

it is perhaps natural that the fears projected onto Freemasonry involve the obtaining of special privileges by an exclu-
sive in-group. The ironic thing is that, in reality, Freemasonry
has long been associated with traditions of egalitarianism
and democracy; the historian Margaret C. Jacob has called
Masonic lodges "schools of government" for their role in
allowing ordinary citizens to practice forms of representa-
tive government before these became the norm in North
America and Western Europe.[75]

At rock bottom, it is significant that two government
investigations have found essentially no real evidence of
Masonic corruption in the English justice system. The heart
of Masonry is not self-aggrandizement or mutual back-
scrubbing. At its best, Masonry really *is* about making good
men better.

SUMMARY

In this chapter, I considered some controversial areas of
Freemasonry. These included the status of women and African Americans within Freemasonry, a personality about
whom many myths gather (Albert Pike), and proposals in

---

75. Jacob, 1991, 2006.

the United Kingdom to require Masons in the justice system and law enforcement to publicly declare themselves.

In terms of its status as an all-male organization, it is important to understand that the underlying mythos of Freemasonry involves all-male groups of ancient and medieval builders and military orders. Because Freemasonry is not properly a place for business networking, its status as an all-male fraternity causes no economic harm to women. At the same time, there are organizations affiliated with Freemasonry that involve women, sometimes to the exclusion of men. There are also organizations outside of the mainstream of Freemasonry that offer their style of initiation directly to women.

African Americans were excluded from mainstream Masonic lodges in the eighteenth through the early twentieth centuries. In the current day, African Americans are welcome in mainstream Masonic lodges in most areas of the United States; it is hoped that the natural course of social progress will remove barriers to Masonic membership for African American men everywhere. Some African American men have formed Prince Hall lodges; most regular American Grand Lodges recognize the Prince Hall lodges as legitimate Masonic lodges, and it is hoped that soon all will.

The nineteeth-century Masonic leader Albert Pike has been accused of involvement with the pro-Confederacy

Knights of the Golden Circle, with the Ku Klux Klan, and with Satanism. However, there is no credible evidence that Pike was ever associated with the KGC or KKK. The supposed Satanist or Luciferian branch of Freemasonry, and Pike's supposed writings in its favor, were all part of an immense hoax perpetrated by an anti-Mason, who later confessed in public.

Following the publication of Stephen Knight's anti-Masonic book *The Brotherhood*, a movement grew to require English Masons in public service to publicly declare themselves. Two government panels found no real evidence of Masonic corruption in public life. The European Convention on Human Rights that became effective in 2000 in England prohibits this sort of discrimination against Freemasons.

7.

Anti-Masonry: Accusations Versus Truths

If one reads up on Freemasonry, either in books or on the Internet, it will not be long before one runs into all kinds of interesting, juicy, scandalous—and completely inaccurate—material about Masonry. Here I shall address a few of the more widespread and egregiously inaccurate accusations. I shall also indicate how some anti-Masonic writers operate, in the hope that the reader will be able to detect these operations as they read other, different accusations.

FREEMASONRY AND RELIGION
IN GENERAL

A great pile of inaccuracies about Freemasonry concerns its relation to religion. I shall mention just a few.

"FREEMASONRY IS A RELIGION": FALSE

First of all, *Freemasonry is not a religion*. All that Masonry has to teach of a doctrinal nature is that God lives; the soul is immortal; all men are should live ethically, morally, and as brothers. This is hardly a religion.

Freemasonry requires that anyone who applies to be a Mason must already hold a belief in a Supreme Being. However, Masonry leaves it up to the individual to consider what the nature of that Supreme Being is. Freemasonry bans all discussion of sectarian religious doctrines in the lodge. Freemasonry is relig*ious*, but is not a relig*ion*.

Yes, Masonry has some religious trappings. Freemasons do conduct group prayer; so do the Boy Scouts of America. Masons have their initiates take their oaths on the Volume of Sacred Law; so usually does the court system when it swears in witnesses. Neither the Scouts nor the courts constitute a religion; neither do the Masons.

"FREEMASONRY SAYS ALL RELIGIONS ARE ALIKE": FALSE

Men of all religious persuasions have equal rights in the lodge; the lodge also bans sectarian religious discussion. Therefore, some people think Freemasonry teaches that all religions are alike. This is utterly untrue.

Freemasonry does not teach that all religions are alike, or equally valid, or anything like that. To the contrary, Freemasonry recognizes that such questions are outside its competence, and that it has no right to say anything at all on these matters.

"FREEMASONRY IS NATURE WORSHIP OR DEISM": FALSE

Some people claim that Masonry is actually a form of nature worship. Others teach that Freemasonry is a form of Deism, a religious position where the Divine Being refrains from interfering in the natural unfolding of the universe. Whether one thinks of the Deist God as an impersonal force (like Nature), or as a personal Being, the Deist God does not grant revelation or produce miracles, and does not intervene in human history; petitionary prayer is a meaningless exercise in a Deist universe. Deism was an important religious position in the early American Republic.[76] However, the idea that Freemasonry teaches Deism is simply false.

Freemasonry neither worships nature nor teaches Deism. Some Masonic symbolism does draw lessons from the natural world, but Masons do not worship nature. Freemasonry makes no specific statements about the personal or impersonal nature of the Supreme Being at all; to do so would be to discuss sectarian religious doctrines, which Freemasons are forbidden to do when they speak as Freemasons. Frankly, Deism would be an odd position for Freemasonry to take, given that Masons offer petitionary prayer during lodge meetings (for example, asking for healing of the sick), and given the Masonic emphasis on the Volume of Sacred Law as a representation of God's revelation to humankind.

FREEMASONRY AND ACCUSATIONS
OF DEVIL WORSHIP

One of the more outrageous accusations made against Freemasonry alleges that Masonry involves devil worship. At the risk of mentioning what would be obvious to any lodge

---

76. Holmes (2006).

member: this accusation is not true in the slightest degree. This accusation is based on a deliberate hoax perpetrated over a century ago—a hoax that the hoaxer revealed himself, during a well-attended press conference.

A nineteenth-century French pornographer, trying to embarrass both the Catholic Church and the Freemasons, wrote volumes of lies for over a decade regarding Freemasonry under the name Léo Taxil (whom we met in our discussion of Albert Pike in Chapter 6). Taxil made incredibly lurid accusations—lodges visited by Satan, statues possessed by demonic spirits in the lodge, and so forth. When his hoax started to unravel, he called a press conference in Paris, attended by representatives of the major French newspapers, and gleefully confessed to the whole thing; he thereby embarrassed the Church, many of whose leaders had hailed Taxil as a hero. (Taxil hated the Church for a variety of reasons. In addition, he briefly had been a Mason, but had been thrown out of the lodge for unmasonic conduct. Thus, anti-Masonry then became the means of his anti-clerical activity.)

Taxil happily confessed his hoax in *1897*.[77] Regrettably, many authors report his accusations as factual today.

---

77. An excellent account of Taxil's hoax and his confession is given in Chapter 2 and Appendix I of de Hoyos and Morris (2004); see also Bernheim, Samii, and Serejski (1996).

FREEMASONRY AND CHRISTIANITY
IN GENERAL

One sometimes hears the notion that Freemasonry is some-how anti-Christian, or incompatible with Christianity. This is totally false.

People seem to get this idea from one of two directions. First, it is true that Freemasons do not permit religious pros-elytizing in the lodge. To some, this seems anti-Christian because they feel that they cannot share their Christian faith in the lodge. Second, it is true that Freemasons do not teach Christianity in the lodge; to some people, this also seems anti-Christian.

All these people miss the point that Masonry is deliber-ately nonsectarian. Freemasonry does not teach Christian-ity because Masonry simply is not a religion. Masonry bans religious discussions in the lodge because the Masonic lodge is supposed to be a place where men of all religious faiths can gather without fear of being called into question for their religious opinions. This is not anti-Christian; if anything, it is pro-religious toleration.

There is a proper time and place to discuss sectarian re-ligious doctrine. That time and place are not within the Masonic lodge, where men of all religions gather.

FREEMASONRY AND THE OCCULT

Another area in which much confusion exists involves Free-masonry and "the occult." This is a bit of a fuzzy area; some writers describe as "occult" anything with which their specific religion disagrees. However, let me try to shed more light than heat in relation to this issue.

Masonic ceremonial does involve the use of an altar, a book representing the Volume of Sacred Law, and candles (or electric lights meant to represent burning tapers). Somehow this says "occult" to some people; what it should say is "ritual." It is a sign of the spiritual impoverishment of our culture that anything ritual seems occult to some.

An organization for Master Masons and their female relatives, the Order of the Eastern Star, does use the symbol of the downward-pointing five-pointed star, also called by some the inverted pentagram. One will occasionally see the five-pointed star used in Masonic symbolism. Some people mistakenly believe that a five-pointed star is a symbol of witchcraft or Satanism.

It is important to understand that the five-pointed star has meant many things to many people over the course of centuries. One can find it on medieval Christian churches in Europe. It appeared as a Christian symbol (symbolizing

the five wounds of Jesus on the cross) during the Middle
Ages. The connection of the five-pointed star with Wicca
seems to be fairly recent.[78] The idea that the inverted pentagram symbolizes evil appears to be the invention of the
nineteenth-century French occultist Eliphas Levi; otherwise, this meaning somehow escaped scholars of the occult
for centuries. The American flag has fifty five-pointed stars;
the American Congressional Medal of Honor even has a
large downward-pointing five-pointed star.[79] In essence,
Freemasonry had five-pointed stars before Wicca, and before such stars (however pointed) became associated with
something evil.

Some Masons see much in Masonic symbolism that is
connected to Kabbalah, a set of esoteric teachings grounded
in Judaism.[80] Some non-Masonic writers consider the Kab-

---

78. Kelly (2007, pp. 103–104) has made the case that Gerald B. Gardner, a
major figure in the establishment of modern Wicca, introduced rituals involving pentagrams/pentacles into Wicca in the 1940s from a variety of
sources, including medieval grimoires and nineteeth- and twentieth-century
handbooks of ritual magic.
79. See the excellent and detailed consideration of the five-pointed star and
Masonry at the website of the Masonic Grand Lodge of British Columbia and
Yukon ("The Pentagram," 2007).
80. See, for example, MacNulty (1991, 1996, 1998).

balah "occult," and so conclude Masonry is "occult" too. The idea that the Kabbalah and Masonry are connected is a matter on which Masons do not agree—but what if this *were* true? There are those outside Masonry who find *any* sort of esoteric teachings "occult," in the sense of being somehow vaguely evil; having these teachings connected with Judaism only makes the teachings more suspect, for the anti-Semite in particular. Kabbalah is a vast and complex domain that has involved many different teachings and practices through the centuries.[81] However, any serious student of Kabbalah can state the following with confidence: there is nothing anti-Christian about Kabbalah; over the centuries, many learned Christians (rightly or wrongly) have thought that Kabbalah is actually a testimony for Christianity;[82] and there is certainly nothing Satanic or evil about Kabbalah.

---

81. See Matt (1995) and Scholem (1978).
82. For example, Reuchlin (1517/1993); see Dan (1997).

FREEMASONRY AND
INTERNATIONAL CONSPIRACY

Freemasonry has been the target of conspiracy theorists for almost three hundred years. I could take up several times the space of this entire book addressing the many things that have been written about Freemasonry and its supposed role in furthering International Conspiracy, along with its supposed involvement in groups and events from the Illuminati and the French Revolution to the New World Order, with everything in between. I just do not have the space in this brief book to do so.

The most terrible things have happened because people believed such things. In the early twentieth century, a bold forgery appeared, *The Protocols of the Elders of Zion*, supposedly the plans of Jews who worked through Masonry to enslave the world.[83] Although the *Protocols* has long been exposed as forgery, it is still published in many countries around the world as truth to this very day. Adolf Hitler

---

83. The *Protocols* is widely available in print and on the Internet. The definitive account of its history, and its nature as a forged document, is given by Cohn (1967). An entertaining, if chilling, account of the *Protocols* and its history is given by Eisner (2005). Zeldis (1998) describes the relevance of the *Protocols* to both anti-Semitism and anti-Masonry.

picked up this theme; he blamed the problems of post–World War I Germany largely on two groups: Jews *and Freemasons.* He then attempted to annihilate both groups of people.[84] Subsequently, in addition to six million Jews, perhaps a quarter of a million Freemasons perished in Nazi concentration camps.

In general, totalitarian regimes have suppressed Freemasonry, whether their orientation is Fascist (Hitler's Germany, Franco's Spain,[85] Mussolini's Italy[86]), Communist (Soviet-era Russia, mainland China), or religious (Iran after 1978). To make matters worse, there are millions of people today worldwide (including in the United States) who believe that the *Protocols* is the truth; they continue to smear Freemasons (and, of course, Jews) every day.

Although I consider the dynamics of beliefs like this in more detail below, I shall make this summary statement here: *Freemasonry is not involved in conspiracy.* Masons ban discussion of partisan politics from the lodge room. Free-

---

84. Hitler believed that Freemasonry was a tool in the hands of the hypothetical Jewish conspiracy to spread religious tolerance and pacifism; see the latter part of Chapter 11 in *Mein Kampf* (Hitler, 1937/2009, pp. 217–218, 222). A recent account of Hitler's persecution of Masonry, focused on German Freemasons, is Melzer (2002). See also "Hitler and Freemasonry" (2010) and "Freemasonry Under the Nazi Regime" (2010).
85. Scanlan (2004).
86. Venzi (2009/2010).

masons concern themselves with personal and inner development, not political power. Masons are not in cahoots
with hostile space aliens to rule the world (as one author
has it), nor are they engaged in a millennia-long project to
enslave humanity (as others claim).

Of course, it is impossible, even in principle, to prove
that a Masonic conspiracy does *not* exist.[87] On the other
hand, it is perfectly reasonable to insist for proof of a claim
that something *does* exist. If someone makes an incendiary
claim—such as claims of a Masonic conspiracy—*insist on
seeing the proof.* That proof had better be something more
than someone else's opinion, or unsupported statement.[88]
As the scientist and educator Carl Sagan once said, "extraordinary claims require extraordinary proof."[89]

---

87. In mathematics, one can prove that something is necessarily *not* so. In
most other fields of inquiry, proving that some category of thing—like Masonic conspiracy—does *not* exist is inherently impossible (see Baggini and
Fosl, 2003, p. 42).
88. Aaronovitch (2010) offers guidelines for the evaluation of conspiracy
theories.
89. See the "Encyclopaedia Galactica" episode of *Cosmos*, originally broad-
cast December 14, 1980, episode no. 12 (at about 1 minute, 24 seconds into
the episode).

FREEMASONRY AND
ROMAN CATHOLICISM

Several myths about Freemasonry specifically involve the Roman Catholic Church. This should not be surprising, given that Grand Lodge Freemasonry arose at a time (the early eighteenth century) when the Roman Catholic Church was a major political power as well as a prominent religious organization (as of course it still is today, although it is less politically powerful).

"FREEMASONRY IS ANTI-CATHOLIC": FALSE

One sometimes hears that Freemasonry is anti-Catholic, or works against the Catholic Church. This is utterly false. I know several past and present Worshipful Masters of lodges who are Roman Catholics. Freemasonry does not involve itself with supporting or working against churches or religions. However, there is a history to this accusation that is worth relating.

During the French Revolution (beginning 1789), Catholic Church property was nationalized, religious orders were suppressed, and priests were required to take oaths of loyalty to the state. In the *Declaration of the Rights of Man and of the Citizen*, the French National Assembly declared religious freedom, and declared all citizens equal, in this country that previously had given special privileges to Catholic clergy ("the First Estate").

Some early conspiracy writers blamed Freemasonry for promoting the French Revolution and its excesses. No real proof was produced to support these accusations; however, French Freemasonry was fragmented across multiple Grand Lodges, some of which departed substantially from mainstream Freemasonry in important ways (a situation that continues today). Freemasonry in France was unable to reject these charges with a united voice, and so many people took the accusations as truth—thus pinning the loss of power of the Catholic Church in France on the Freemasons. It is noteworthy that in pre-Revolutionary France, it is said that there were lodges entirely made up of Catholic clergy,[90] which would suggest that the idea that Masonry was anti-Catholic is unfounded.

Switching our focus to Italy, it is well-known that two nineteenth-century Italian Freemasons, Giuseppe Mazzini (1805–1872) and Giuseppe Garibaldi (1807–1882), were instrumental in forging a united Italy out of a patchwork of partitions that had left the boot of Italy divided among

---

90. "Freemasons in the French Revolution" (2002).

various major and minor European powers. However, this unification was accomplished, in part, at the expense of the Papal States. The Freemason Simón Bolívar (1783–1830) was also instrumental in Latin American independence movements, which also succeeded, to some extent, at the expense of the political power of the Catholic Church.

Thus, the idea that Freemasonry works against Roman Catholicism largely comes about because of famous Masons being involved in various movements for independence and democracy. Freemasonry in its many branches has long been a proponent of tolerance of different religions and the separation of church and state—both of which positions are perceived by some, falsely, as especially anti-Catholic.

"CATHOLICS MAY NOT BECOME FREEMASONS": FALSE

One also sometimes hears that Catholics may not become Freemasons. This is a complex question, although overall it is still the case that this is false.

As far as Freemasonry is concerned, members of any religion are eligible to become Masons, along with "unchurched" believers in a Supreme Being. There are many Roman Catholic Freemasons. It is as simple as that. (Typically, candidates for Freemasonry are not even asked what their specific religions are.)

It is true, however, that over the last three hundred years some popes have issued formal declarations against what they thought was Freemasonry. The broadest was probably the encyclical *Humanum Genus*, promulgated by Pope Leo XIII in 1884, in which the pope condemned Freemasonry in no uncertain terms—largely on the grounds that Freemasonry encouraged the separation of church and state, freedom of religion, public education, and democracy.[91]

This is a complicated issue that I can address only briefly here. My sense of the situation is that the popes of today have come to see that democracy, the separation of church and state, and public education are not the threats to Roman Catholicism that they appeared to be in 1884. Thus, we see that the papal condemnations of Freemasonry are based on an inaccurate image of the fraternity. Many Catholic Masons, at the least, seem to feel that these papal condemnations, based as they are on a faulty understanding of Masonry, are not binding for Catholics today.

---

91. The Vatican's English translation of *Humanum Genus* is available online (*Humanum Genus*, n.d.). A full translation of *Humanum Genus* is found in Robinson (1989); see especially pp. 307–311, 349, 350, 352–353. A full translation, with the reply of Albert Pike, a nineteenth-century Masonic leader, is given in "The Letter . . ." (1962); see especially pp. 10, 11, 13.

Another set of issues involves a report issued by the German [Roman Catholic] Bishops Conference in 1980.[92] The bishops objected to Freemasonry on the basis of a dozen characteristics of Masonry—none of which actually describe Freemasonry accurately, at least as it is practiced in the mainstream.[93] Here again, Catholics may feel justified in thinking that objections based on the German Bishops Conference report are ultimately groundless.

SOME THOUGHTS ON ANTI-MASONRY

Why do people believe anti-Masonic accusations, particularly those of the more outrageous variety? Now we get into the psychology of conspiracy. To answer this question properly, we would need to consider the dynamics of scapegoating and demonization.[94] Here, I shall just touch on some major points.

---

92. This report is described in detail by Jenkins (1996).
93. Until my anticipated book-length treatment of this issue is completed, I refer readers to a series of posts that I wrote regarding this subject on my blog, Freemasonry: Reality, Myth, and Legend (Koltko-Rivera, 2009).
94. An excellent and detailed description of these dynamics in relation to anti-Masonic conspiracy theories is offered by the sociologist Chip Berlet (2002).

Conspiracy theories make things *simple*. There is no need to consider subtle or complex factors behind economic or social unrest, no need to take into account the unsettling reality that bad things in the world sometimes happen without planning, no need to engage reason and rationality. Just focus on the conspiracy and blame it all on Them.

Conspiracy theories also make life *easy*. Anti-Masonic conspiracy theories allow people to avoid the difficult work of educating themselves, participating in the democratic process, and creating social, political, and economic change; why bother, when They are running everything from behind the scenes? Rather than taking personal responsibility to make the world a better place, it is so much easier to find an external scapegoat for the world's problems.

Masons—with their history of being the targets of outrageous accusations like Taxil's, and with their tradition of Masonic privacy—are ready candidates for scapegoating. In addition, Masons have long preached religious tolerance and the use of reason in the political process. This has earned Freemasonry the enmity of those religious and political authorities who rely on intolerance and fear- or emotion-based appeals to their followers.

Some readers will be able to investigate these issues quite directly; they have family members or friends who are Free-

masons. If you are concerned about issues like devil worship or international conspiracy, I suggest that you simply
ask the Freemasons you know quite directly about these
issues. Be prepared to receive a few odd looks. However,
your Masonic friends and relatives—once they realize that
you are serious—will tell you the truth: Freemasons simply have nothing to do with such things. "Ah," some anti-
Masons will say, "that's because *those* Masons are too low in
the hierarchy to *know!* The *true* leadership of the organization knows the *real* truth."

Really? That is interesting—because it would be a mon-
umentally stupid way to run a conspiracy.

People spend years in Freemasonry learning to revere
such scriptures as the Bible, live as gentlemen, uphold constitutional freedoms, show respect to people of different
religions, and so forth. Then—to hear some conspiracy
theorists tell the story—all of a sudden, when Masons become part of the inner circle of Masonic leadership, they
are supposed to throw all that away and either worship the
devil, plot to enslave humanity, or both. An organization
that worked at such cross-purposes with itself would not
survive thirty years, let alone three hundred.

There is another fatal problem with the notion that the
real purpose of Masonry is only known to the high leadership. There *is* no high leadership in Freemasonry. The high-

est authority over the local lodge is the Grand Lodge of the state—say, Iowa. There simply is no overarching body that gives orders to the U.S. State Grand Lodges. Yes, there are those thirty-third-degree Masons, but the thirty-third degree is an honor in the Scottish Rite, an organization not founded until Grand Lodge Freemasonry was over eighty years old, and to which only a minority of Masons belong.

One will not learn much accurate information about Freemasonry from its detractors, anymore than one would expect to learn much accurate information about Jews from the Nazis, or about African Americans from the Ku Klux Klan. If you have questions about Freemasonry, drop by your local lodge and ask someone there. In addition, there are some good websites that have been developed by Freemasons to respond to anti-Masonry, such as the top-notch site developed by the Grand Lodge of British Columbia and Yukon[95] and the excellent site titled Anti-Masonry Points of View.[96] See my suggestions for further reading regarding anti-Masonry in Chapter 8.

---

95. http://www.freemasonry.bcy.ca/texts/index.html.
96. http://www.masonicinfo.com/.

SUMMARY

Freemasonry is not a religion, let alone a devil-worshipping religion. It is not Deism, not nature worship, and not anti-Christian, either. Freemasonry is not involved in what is popularly called "the occult," nor in international conspiracy. Freemasonry does not work against the Roman Catholic Church, and it welcomes Roman Catholics as Masons. The condemnations of Freemasonry issued by papal or other Catholic authorities are built upon inaccurate understandings of Masonry and its activities. Freemasonry is a convenient scapegoat for conspiracy theorists, but in fact it has no high leadership or inner circle that could work to enslave humanity in secret—an activity that would be a serious violation of Masonic morality in any event.

8.

Freemasonry in Fiction: Myth Versus Reality

Freemasonry occasionally shows up in novels and motion pictures. However, media depictions of Masonry often leave something to be desired. Below, I consider a few recent appearances of Masonry in popular fiction and indicate the differences between myth and reality.

FROM HELL
(GRAPHIC NOVEL, 1999; MOVIE, 2001)

From Hell claims that the Jack the Ripper murders of the nineteenth century were committed and abetted by Freemasons, who also supposedly concealed the identity of the Ripper. The graphic novel *From Hell* was coauthored by popular writer Alan Moore (the coauthor of the immensely popular *Watchmen*); the movie version starred Johnny Depp and Heather Graham. Of course, names like these ensured a wide distribution for this book and movie, and the ideas behind them.

There is no truth to these notions. Accounts of a Masonic conspiracy in the Ripper case have their primary source solely in statements made by Joseph Sickert (also known as Joseph Gorman) to the journalist Stephen Knight, who used these statements as the basis for Knight's 1976 book *Jack the Ripper: The Final Solution*.[97] However, two years later, Sickert/Gorman publicly admitted that "it was a hoax; I made it all up. . . . a whopping fib."[98]

For his part, Alan Moore admitted that "Knight's theory has been roundly attacked and derided in recent times, and indeed there are grounds for supposing that much of [Knight's book] *Final Solution* may have been intended as an ingenious hoax."[99] In *From Hell*, Moore even describes the controversy involving Sickert's then-decade-old con-

---

97. Knight (1976/1982). The theory is also described in Knight (1984/1986, pp. 52–55).
98. D. May (1978). Knight (1978) rejected Sickert's confession.
99. Moore and Campbell (1989/2006), Appendix I, p. 1, comment on Chapter 1.

fession to this hoax regarding the Masons.[100] However, none of this stopped Moore from using Sickert's original fabrications as the core of *From Hell*.

In sum, *From Hell* does not depict the real story of the Ripper murders, nor the reality of Freemasonry.[101] As Alan Moore himself put it:

> Truth is, this has never been about the murders, nor the killer nor his victims. It's about us. About our minds and how they dance. Jack mirrors our hysterias. Faceless, he is the receptacle for each new social panic. He's a Jew, a Doctor, a Freemason or a wayward Royal.[102]

THE LEAGUE OF EXTRAORDINARY GENTLEMEN
(COMIC BOOK, 1999; MOVIE, 2003)

Alan Moore also coauthored a limited series comic book, later made into an action adventure movie starring Sean Connery. In his comic, author Moore, ever the friend to the

---

100. Moore and Campbell (1989/2006), Appendix II, pp. 13–15.
101. A thorough examination of the myth of Masonic involvement in the Ripper case is given by Bessel (2001).
102. Moore and Campbell (1989/2006), Appendix II, p. 22.

Freemasons, depicts the Masons as the power behind the entire government of England, and a sinister power, at that. Moore also used Masonic symbolism to mark the clothes and buildings of his bad guys in his sequel comics, *The League of Extraordinary Gentlemen, Volume II* (collected edition, 2003) and *The League of Extraordinary Gentlemen: Black Dossier* (issued as a graphic novel, 2007).

The reality is that, although there long have been members of the British royal family involved in the fraternity, Masonry is not the power behind the throne of that or any other country. I have heard it suggested that Alan Moore is simply putting the Freemasons in such a sinister light as a plot device. How very thoughtful of him.

THE DA VINCI CODE
(NOVEL, 2003; MOVIE, 2006)

This phenomenally successful book claims that the medieval Knights Templar concealed the bloodline of Jesus and Mary Magdalene; there are subtle hints (Chapters 48 and 56) that Masons were involved. Not true!

Dan Brown, the novel's author, based a lot of his backstory on claims made in various highly speculative and controversial books. Many of the claims reported in *those* books—for example, material regarding the Priory of Sion—have been found to be based on forged documents; essentially, the authors were taken in by others. As for the involvement of Masonry in concealing this purported bloodline: there is just no credible evidence for it.

NATIONAL TREASURE
(MOVIE, 2004)

This movie showed Freemasonry in a positive light in relation to the founding of the American Republic. It *is* true that many of the Founding Fathers were Freemasons. However, it is *not* true that the Founding Fathers coded secret Masonic messages onto the Declaration of Independence. Nor did the Knights Templar bury ballrooms full of gold treasure in lower Manhattan. The movie is a very enjoyable adventure story, not a historical documentary.

NATIONAL TREASURE: BOOK OF SECRETS
(MOVIE, 2007)

This movie focuses on the Lincoln assassination. Freemasonry is again a part of the backstory. In a couple of scenes of the original script (deleted from the movie as released in theaters), the film addresses that favorite bugaboo of the conspiracy theorists, the legendary thirty-third-degree Masons who supposedly are in on every important secret.

There really are thirty-third-degree Masons. This is an honor given to Scottish Rite Masons (see Chapter 3) who have given years of service to humanity, to Masonry, or to the Scottish Rite. (For example, the first American astronaut to orbit the earth and a former U.S. senator, the Honorable John H. Glenn, Jr., had conferred upon him the thirty-third degree.)

I have had the pleasure of knowing dozens of men who hold the thirty-third degree. Several of them are my friends; I know some who are very accomplished in their chosen fields. However, they are no more privy to the secrets of the world than anyone else.

THE LOST SYMBOL
(NOVEL, 2009)

Dan Brown's long-awaited sequel to *The Da Vinci Code* centered on a conspiracy involving Freemasonry—but a *benign* conspiracy, to protect and maintain a secret that literally has the power to transform humanity. There are minor peccadilloes one could note regarding the accuracy of Brown's depiction of the externals and mechanics of Freemasonry and its history. However, overall, Brown did an excellent job of portraying the values of Freemasonry correctly. (As I mentioned near the end of Chapter 3, Dan Brown chose to focus on Freemasonry because of its tradition of religious tolerance.)

9.

How to Become a Freemason

If someone wished to become a Freemason, how would he go about doing that? There may be minor variations between one Grand Lodge jurisdiction and another, but the basic process will be the same throughout:

- Establish eligibility.
- Find the local lodge.
- Get to know some of the local lodge brothers.
- File a petition.
- Meet with the Investigation Committee.
- Undergo the "trial of the ballot box."
- Receive the degrees of Freemasonry.

I describe each step below. However, I emphasize that these steps only apply to a person if indeed he has the desire to become a Freemason. Masons do not recruit; I am not recruiting here. *If* one feels the desire—if Freemasonry "calls" to a person, if you will—then, and only then, does the following apply to any individual.

ESTABLISH ELIGIBILITY

The very basic eligibility requirements for a candidate for Freemasonry are straightforward. The candidate must:

- be male;
- hold a belief in a Supreme Being and the immortality of the human soul;
- be of age (a minimum of twenty-one years of age in many jurisdictions, eighteen or nineteen in others, especially if the man is a DeMolay alumnus or the son of a Mason);
- be physically and mentally capable of participating in and understanding the Masonic degrees;
- be interested in Freemasonry on its own merits and

not have the intent of gaining some sort of advantage in business or the social world;

- be freeborn of freeborn parents (earlier generations do not matter for this issue); and
- be of good moral character. (This is not boilerplate. Felony convictions are not looked upon kindly in a potential candidate for Freemasonry.)

Incidentally, it is worth emphasizing that these characteristics apply to the candidate, but not to the candidate's ancestors. Quite frankly, my own late father could not have met all these qualifications. That was completely immaterial to my lodge, which simply could not have cared less—I was the one applying, not my father.

Should a candidate find that he is eligible, the next step is finding his local lodge. There are well over 10,000 lodges in the United States, so it is likely that there is one not far from the candidate.

FIND THE LOCAL LODGE

The easiest way for a candidate to find his local lodge would be to simply ask any of his acquaintances who happen to be

Masons where the local lodge is. However, if the candidate is like I was, and does not know anyone who is a Mason, then he must try other methods.

A candidate might try the classified ("yellow pages") telephone directory under "Fraternal Organizations." One should look for a listing like "Winter Park Lodge No. 239, F&AM," or "McAllen Lodge No. 1110, AF&AM," with other lodge names and numbers, of course. The letters at the end stand for "Free and Accepted Masons" and "Ancient Free and Accepted Masons," and identify the lodges involved as "regular" members of their state Grand Lodges. (Different states just came to have different customs on the wording. Winter Park is in Florida, McAllen in Texas. In South Carolina, the abbreviation is "A.F.M."; in Washington, D.C., it is "F.A.A.M.") Of course, individuals interested in, for example, lodges of the Prince Hall Affiliation (see Chapter 6) would look for the letters "PHA."

This lettering actually matters. Anybody can call themselves a Masonic lodge. What Masons call "regular" lodges are those that can ultimately trace themselves back to the original Grand Lodges of England. These are the F&AM and so forth lodges, as I described above; as I note in Chapter 6, increasing numbers of American Grand Lodges recognize that the Prince Hall Affiliation is regular as well. Other lodge organizations are called "clandestine," and typically have very dubious origins (often being the off-spring of egotism and schism). Thus I suggest that someone interested in the mainstream Masonic experience would do well to confine himself to regular lodges.

One might check with the Grand Lodge of one's area. (In the United States, there is a separate Grand Lodge for each state, the District of Columbia, and Puerto Rico.) One might type the following phrase into an Internet search engine: "Grand Lodge of [*name of one's state*]." Usually, the first result to appear will be the website of one's Grand Lodge. On the Grand Lodge website, the candidate will find a listing of all the lodges under the jurisdiction of his Grand Lodge. He may need to dig around a bit and look at actual addresses; many lodges have names—like "Solomon's Lodge"—that do not explain where they are located.

The Grand Lodge listing will usually state when a lodge meets. The directory will at least give a telephone number, and often both a physical and an e-mail address as well. One might either drop by or call the lodge, about an hour or so before it meets, and find out when one can come by to visit with some of the lodge brothers.

If there are several lodges within one's community, one might take down contact information for each of them. Different lodges have different flavors; the candidate may find that he gravitates more toward the brothers of one lodge than another. The candidate should feel free to shop around and visit more than one lodge.

GET TO KNOW SOME OF THE LOCAL LODGE BROTHERS

Many lodges have an open dinner an hour or so before the official lodge meeting begins; often this dinner is held before only one of the two monthly meetings, if there are two. Alternatively, some lodges have a dinner or "collation" after the lodge meeting. A candidate should try to attend this dinner one or more times for any lodge he is seriously interested in joining. He should get to know the fellows there, and find out at which lodge he feels most comfortable. The candidate should not be bashful about asking the lodge brothers any questions he might have, either about Freemasonry in general or about their specific lodge.

FILE A PETITION

The next step is to file a formal petition for the degrees of Freemasonry. (There are many terms that have a special meaning within Freemasonry, and "petition" is one of them; it is an application.) The candidate must have this petition sponsored by, typically, two or three members of the lodge to which he is applying. (The acquaintances he has made at the lodge dinners would probably be happy to sign as sponsors.) There will be fees, clearly indicated, to apply for the degrees and for the lodge dues. Depending on the Grand Lodge, the candidate may be asked for the names and addresses of two or three individuals (not those sponsoring him, and not necessarily Masons, either) who can be contacted to write letters of recommendation with regard to the character of the candidate.

The candidate will be asked a number of questions on the petition. He will be asked whether he holds a belief in a Supreme Being. He will also be asked whether he has experienced any criminal convictions; if he has, he will be asked for details. One should be honest in answering these questions. It is conceivable that a lodge might be willing to overlook a youthful lapse of judgment.

MEET WITH THE INVESTIGATION COMMITTEE

After the candidate files his petition, he (and his significant other, if any) will be asked to meet with a committee of two or three brothers from the lodge, the Investigation Committee. The committee will meet with the candidate at a place and time of his convenience, either at his home or another place of his choice. This is an opportunity for the candidate and his significant other to ask any questions that the two of them may have about Freemasonry. In addition, the Committee will wish to confirm that the candidate holds a belief in a Supreme Being, and so forth. The Committee will then make its recommendation in private to the lodge.

Could the Investigation Committee recommend that the lodge reject a candidate? Of course it could. However, one would expect that this would happen relatively infrequently. Most of the people whom a committee would reject outright—those who clearly do not meet the qualifications listed at the beginning of this chapter—are unlikely to be petitioning for Freemasonry anyway. However, the lodge does have the moral responsibility to conduct this investigation and to confirm the basic eligibility of every candidate.

After the report of the Investigation Committee to the lodge, and assuming that the report is favorable, the lodge is required to let the candidate's petition "lay over" without taking action on it, typically for a month. The lodge then votes on the petition.

UNDERGOING THE
"TRIAL OF THE BALLOT BOX"

Bringing in a new member of the lodge is a happy occasion, but it is also a solemn matter. Once a man is brought in, unless he commits an egregious offense (such as a felony), or stops paying dues, he is entitled to remain a member of that lodge for the rest of his life. That can be a very long time. Consequently, a lodge wants to be sure, at the very beginning of a man's Masonic involvement, that he will not bring disharmony into the lodge. Hence, what Masons call the "trial of the ballot box."

About a month after the Investigation Committee makes its report to the lodge about a candidate, the lodge will vote on that candidate's petition. In most jurisdictions, for a candidate to be accepted for initiation, the vote must be unanimous in the affirmative. (In some jurisdictions, one or even two negative votes still allow admission; this is still election by an enormous landslide.)

Are candidates ever rejected at the ballot box? Yes, it happens—not most of the time, but it does happen. Freemasons are forbidden to describe how they voted, or why they voted a certain way, so it is difficult to tell why candidates are occasionally rejected. In the case of rejection, the candidate receives a refund of fees and dues paid; he may be eligible to reapply, to that lodge or another, in about a year, in many jurisdictions.

RECEIVE THE
DEGREES OF FREEMASONRY

Soon after the lodge votes affirmatively on a candidate's petition, the secretary of the lodge will inform him of a date for his initiation. A Masonic degree is a production, so it is not unusual for lodges to pull together a small number of candidates into one group that experiences initiation together on the same evening. Thus, the candidate's initiation may occur a couple of months after the lodge conducts balloting on his petition. (Occasionally, lodges have waiting lists of candidates for initiation.)

The candidate should come dressed nicely for his initiation. I suggest a jacket and tie and so forth; some lodges prefer a tuxedo.

The three degrees of initiation are conducted separately, typically with at least a month between the ceremonies. Thus, it will take some months to receive the three foundational degrees of Freemasonry.

It is typical for candidates who have received a degree to

be required to "deliver proof of their proficiency" in that degree before proceeding to the next degree. (This is an echo of the customs of the stonemasons, who had to demonstrate their proficiency in working with stone before moving beyond the apprentice stage.) The nature of the proficiency differs across jurisdictions and lodges. In some lodges, proficiency is demonstrated by reciting a "catechism" or summary of the degree from memory. (Brethren are assigned to work with candidates to help them memorize the material.) In other jurisdictions, proficiency is demonstrated by writing essays on Masonic symbolism. Some lodges require both types of demonstration of proficiency.

AFTER RECEIVING THE THREE BASIC DEGREES OF FREEMASONRY

After a man becomes a Master Mason, he is as much of a Mason as anyone else. There are many paths to take in Masonry from that point; one may take more than one. These paths may involve service in the local lodge, or further degrees, or activity in affiliated organizations (see Chapter 3).

One's initiation would be a great time to write a journal entry. The candidate might reflect on the feelings he had upon going through initiation. There is a paradox here: on

the one hand, men have received the degrees of Freemasonry in substantially the same form as the candidate did for
perhaps three centuries; on the other hand, no one else will
have had quite the same experience as he has. That special
experience, individual to the candidate, is one of the legitimate mysteries of Freemasonry, and one of its real secrets.

10.

Learning More About Freemasonry

This book is only a relatively brief introduction to Freemasonry. Some readers, whether they ever become Masons or not, will wish to delve further into the subject. There is much literature available, to be sure. For example, one may consider longer, more detailed introductions. One can study the symbolism of Freemasonry. The history of Freemasonry is certainly fascinating (if sometimes puzzling). There is certainly a great deal that one *might* study—but thereby hangs a problem.

There are probably tens of thousands of books on Freemasonry (not including those on anti-Masonry). Not all of them are of high quality. Some are quite speculative, some are based on poor research. Some authors assume that the reader already knows a great deal about Freemasonry before beginning to read their books.

The challenge, then, is to know what is worthwhile to read—that is, what is accurate, interesting, and appropriate to read for someone just learning about Freemasonry. Below, I make suggestions that I think fit these qualifications. In particular, I describe some books that (1) provide a further introduction to Freemasonry, (2) consider Masonic symbolism, (3) address Masonic history, and (4) respond to anti-Masonry. I list the books *very* roughly in the order in which I think they would be useful to the reader.

INTRODUCTIONS TO FREEMASONRY

I have a determined preference for introductions to Freemasonry that are written by actual Freemasons. The best of these include the following.

- W. Kirk MacNulty. *Freemasonry: Symbols, Secrets, Significance.* New York: Thames & Hudson, 2006.
- Christopher Hodapp. *Freemasons for Dummies.* Hoboken, NJ: Wiley, 2005.
- S. Brent Morris. *The Complete Idiot's Guide to Freemasonry.* New York: Alpha/Penguin, 2006.

- Jay Kinney. *The Masonic Myth: Unlocking the Truth About the Symbols, the Secret Rites, and the History of Freemasonry.* New York: HarperCollins, 2009.

MASONIC SYMBOLISM

- W. Kirk MacNulty. *Freemasonry: A Journey Through Ritual and Symbol.* New York: Thames & Hudson, 1991.
- ———. *Freemasonry: Symbols, Secrets, Significance.* New York: Thames & Hudson, 2006.

MASONIC HISTORY

- Angel Millar. *Freemasonry: A History.* San Diego, CA: Thunder Bay Press/Advantage Publishers Group, 2005.
- Jasper Ridley. *The Freemasons: A History of the World's Most Powerful Secret Society.* New York: Arcade Publishing, 2001.

RESPONSES TO ANTI-MASONRY

- Arturo de Hoyos and S. Brent Morris. *Is It True What They Say About Freemasonry? The Methods of Anti-Masons.* New York: M. Evans, 2004. This is particularly good about accusations made by some specific anti-Masonic authors, such as John Ankerberg and Jim Shaw.
- John J. Robinson. *A Pilgrim's Path: Freemasonry and the Religious Right.* New York: M. Evans, 1993.
- Arturo de Hoyos. *Cloud of Prejudice: A Study in Anti-Masonry* (rev. ed.). Kila, MT: Kessinger, 1993.

These books are a good start. Good luck to you in your Masonic studies.

GLOSSARY

Appendant Body. An Appendant Body is an organization that requires that its members be Master Masons, or be a familial relative of a Master Mason. To be recognized as legitimate, such organizations must be approved by the Grand Lodge of Masons in which they operate. Examples of Appendant Bodies include the *York Rite* and the *Scottish Rite*. Appendant Bodies are sometimes called "Concordant Bodies."

Blue Lodge. The Blue Lodge is the organizational unit at the foundation of Freemasonry. It is a *Lodge* that confers the three basic Masonic *degrees*.

Clandestine Freemasonry. Members of lodges within *Regular Freemasonry* call other forms of Freemasonry Clandestine Freemasonry. Some clandestine lodges are alternative forms of Freemasonry that have been around for over a century. Some are the creations of people, angry at some perceived slight in a regular lodge, who dealt with their issues by breaking off into a separate organization of their own devising. Some were formed by people who were actually expelled from regular lodges.

Yet others were created by people who learned about Masonry from books and decided to create a lodge without ever having been a member of a regular lodge. Let the would-be initiate beware.

Degree. A degree is a level of initiation. Thus, we refer to the *three basic degrees* of Freemasonry, also known as the *Blue Lodge* degrees: the First Degree (1°) or Entered Apprentice, the Second Degree (2°) or Fellow Craft, and the Third Degree (3°) or Master Mason. *High degree* bodies, such as the *York Rite* and the *Scottish Rite*, offer further degrees to Master Masons.

East. This is a symbolic direction that has ritual importance within Freemasonry. Where the Worshipful Master of a lodge has his chair is always the (Masonic) East, regardless of what a magnetic compass would say.

F&AM Lodges. "F&AM," standing for "Free and Accepted Masons," along with some accepted variants (see Chapter 9) is a designation used by *Regular Lodges.*

Freemasonry. Freemasonry is a fraternity that uses ceremonies of initiation to teach symbolic lessons about philosophy, morality, and character. The different components of this definition are explained in Chapter 1.

Grand Lodge. This is the highest unit of organization within *Blue Lodge* Freemasonry. The Grand Lodge directs the work of all local *Lodges* within its jurisdiction. In the United States, there is a Grand Lodge for each of the fifty States, plus the District of Columbia and Puerto Rico. (Most *F&AM* Grand Lodges recognize the concurrent jurisdiction of a Prince Hall Grand Lodge functioning within their states as well.) Outside the United States, a single *regular* Grand Lodge typically functions at the national level (for example, in England). Some countries have more than one Grand Lodge, either because different territories within the country each has its own Grand Lodge (as in Australia), or because there are overlapping Grand Lodges that recognize each other as regular.

High degree Freemasonry. This is the name given to organizations that offer degrees that in some way build upon the three foundational degrees of the *Blue Lodge*. Examples are the *York Rite* and the *Scottish Rite*.

Initiate. One who has experienced *initiation*.

Initiation. Initiation is a ritual activity through which people are imparted certain teachings confidentially, are made part of a group, and become people who are in some way different from who they were before initiation. I consider the nature of initiation in Chapters 1 and 2.

Jurisdiction. See *Grand Lodge*.

Lodge(s). The term "Lodge" may refer to (1) a local group of Masons who meet as a single unit, or (2) the building in which they meet. Sometimes the term is used metaphorically to refer to all of Freemasonry.

Masonic. Of or pertaining to Freemasonry.

Order of the Eastern Star. An *Appendant Body* for both Master Masons and their female relatives.

Petition. An application to become a Freemason, or a member of an *Appendant Body*.

Prince Hall Affiliation/Freemasonry. A form of Freemasonry descending from a *Lodge* of African Americans, initiated by a British military *Lodge* in 1775. (See Chapter 6.)

Regular Freemasonry. The term "regular" refers to Masonic lodges and *Grand Lodges* that ultimately derive from the predecessors of the United Grand Lodge of England. This includes the *F&AM Lodges* of the United States, and many other lodges around the world. Many American Lodges now recognize *Prince Hall Affiliation* Lodges as regular. (Non-regular lodges are referred to by regular lodges as *Clandestine.*)

Rite. A system that presents a collection of *degrees* in an organized fashion is a Rite. Examples include the *Scottish Rite* and the *York Rite.*

Scottish Rite. A *high degree* organization that offers additional *degrees* to Master Masons. In the United States, there are two Scottish Rite organizations, the Southern Jurisdiction and the Northern Masonic Jurisdiction. The Scottish Rite offers from the fourth degree to the thirty-second degree. (The thirty-third degree is awarded as an honor to especially dedicated Masons.) However, this sequence, fourth through thirty-third, is only recognized within the Scottish Rite. Thus, the common misconception that the thirty-third-degree Masons are the highest-level Masons is utterly false.

Volume of Sacred Law ("VLS"). This is a book of sacred writings that must be open on the altar of the lodge room whenever a Masonic *Lodge* meets. In the United States, the VLS is usually represented by the King James edition of the Holy Bible; in some jurisdictions, this Bible is stipulated as "the" *VLS.*

Warden, Senior or Junior. These are the second and third officers, respectively, of a *Blue Lodge.*

Worshipful Master. This is the chief officer of a *Blue Lodge.* The term "Worshipful" is an archaic English term denoting "Worthy of Respect." (Some

British civil officials, such as mayors, still have this word applied to them.) No one directs religious worship to the Worshipful Master of a *lodge*.

York Rite. A *high degree* organization that offers additional *degrees* to Master Masons. The York Rite is actually a loose confederation of three separate organizations, representing the Chapter of Royal Arch Masons, the Council of Royal and Select Masters, and the Commandery of the Knights Templar.

REFERENCES

Note: The full name of the annual publication, *Heredom*, is *Heredom: The Transactions of the Scottish Rite Research Society*; many Masonic libraries have copies, which can also be obtained directly from the Society: http://www.scottishrite.org/what/educ/srrs.html. The term "GL-BCY" stands for "the Grand Lodge of British Columbia and Yukon, AF&AM." *Freemasonry Today* is the official journal of the United Grand Lodge of England; issues may be consulted online at http://www.freemasonrytoday.com/.

Aaronovitch, David. 2010. *Voodoo Histories: The Role of the Conspiracy Theory in Shaping Modern History*. New York: Riverhead Books.

"Abel Claren de la Rive (1855–1914)." 2001. Accessed February 11, 2010, http://www.freemasonry.bcy.ca/anti-masonry/delarive.html.

Armstrong, Karen. 2001. *Holy War: The Crusades and Their Impact on Today's World* (revised edition). New York: Anchor Books.

Baggini, J., and P.S. Fosl. 2003. *The Philosopher's Toolkit*. Malden, MA: Blackwell.

Barber, Malcolm. 1994. *The New Knighthood: A History of the Order of the Temple*. Cambridge: Cambridge University Press.

Barnstone, Willis (ed.). 2005. *The Other Bible: Jewish Pseudepigrapha, Christian Apocrypha, Gnostic Scriptures, Kabbalah, Dead Sea Scrolls*. New York: HarperCollins.

Batham, Cyril N. 1992. "Ramsay's Oration: The Epernay and Grand Lodge Version," *Heredom* 1: 49–59. Originally published in *Ars Quatuor Coronatorum* 81 (1968).

Bauer, Alain. 2007. *Isaac Newton's Freemasonry: The Alchemy of Science and Mysticism*. Rochester, VT: Inner Traditions.

Berlet, Chip. 2002. "Anti-Masonic Conspiracy Theories: A Narrative Form of Demonization and Scapegoating," *Heredom* 10: 243–75.

Bernheim, Alain, and Arturo de Hoyos. 2006. "Introduction to the Rituals of the Rite of Strict Observance," *Heredom* 14: 47–104.

Bernheim, A., A. W. Samii, and E. Serejski. 1996. "The Confession of Léo Taxil," *Heredom* 5: 137–68, http://www.freemasonry.bcy.ca/texts/taxil_confessed.html.

Bessel, Paul M. 2001. "The 'Jack the Ripper' Murders: An Examination of Alleged Masonic Connections," *Heredom* 9: 53–67.

Brown, Walter Lee. 1997. *A Life of Albert Pike*. Fayetteville: The University of Arkansas Press.

Burkert, Walter. 1985. *Greek Religion*. Cambridge, MA: Harvard University Press.

Charles, R. H. 2003. *The Book of Enoch the Prophet*. York Beach, ME: Weiser. Originally published 1912.

Churton, Tobias. 1998. "Letter from the Editor," *Freemasonry Today* 4, http://www.freemasonrytoday.com/04/p01.php.

———. 2002. *The Golden Builders: Alchemists, Rosicrucians, and the First Freemasons*. York Beach, ME: Red Wheel/ Weiser.

———. 2006. *The Magus of Freemasonry: The Mysterious Life of Elias*

Ashmole: Scientist, Alchemist, and Founder of the Royal Society. Rochester, VT: Inner Traditions.

Cohn, Norman. 1967. *Warrant for Genocide: The Myth of the Jewish World-Conspiracy and the Protocols of the Elders of Zion.* London: Eyre & Spottiswoode.

Coil, Henry Wilson; William Moseley Brown, William L. Cummings, Harold Van Buren Voorhis, and Allen E. Roberts, eds. 1996. *Coil's Masonic Encyclopedia* (revised edition). Richmond, VA: Macoy Publishing and Supply Company.

Crenshaw, Ollinger. 1941. "The Knights of the Golden Circle: The Career of George Bickley," *American Historical Review* 47(1): 23–50.

Dan, Joseph. 1993. *The Ancient Jewish Mysticism.* Tel Aviv, Israel: MOD.

———, ed. 1997. *The Christian Kabbalah: Jewish Mystical Books and Their Christian Interpreters.* Cambridge, MA: Harvard College Library.

de Hoyos, Arturo, ed. 2008. *Albert Pike's "ESOTERIKA": The Symbolism of the Blue Degrees of Freemasonry* (2nd ed.). Washington, D.C.: The Scottish Rite Research Society.

——— and S. Brent Morris. 2004. *Is It True What They Say About Freemasonry? The Methods of Anti-Masons.* New York: M. Evans.

Dewan, Sheila, and Robbie Brown. July 3, 2009. "Black Member Tests Message of Masons in Georgia Lodges," *The New York Times,* p. A15, http://www.nytimes.com/2009/07/03/us/03masons.html.

Dunn, Roy Sylvan. 1967. "The KGC in Texas," *Southwestern Historical Quarterly* 70: 543–73.

Eisner, Will. 2005. *The Plot: The Secret Story of The Protocols of the Elders of Zion.* New York: Norton.

Exner, John E., Jr. 2003. *The Rorschach: A Comprehensive System* (Vol. 1, 4th ed.). Hoboken, NJ: Wiley.

Fanning, Philip Ashley. 2009. *Isaac Newton and the Transmutation of*

Alchemy: An Alternate View of the Scientific Revolution. Berkeley, CA: North Atlantic Books.

Focus. December 2009. Accessed February 11, 2010, http://www.msana .com/focusdec09.asp.

"Freemasonry in the Police and the Judiciary." March 19, 1997. Excerpt from Third Report of the 1996–1997 Session of the Select Committee on Home Affairs, House of Commons, http://www.charlton.demon .co.uk/masonic/report.html.

"Freemasonry in Public Life." May 25, 1999. Second Report of the 1998–1999 Session of the Select Committee on Home Affairs, House of Commons, http://www.parliament.the-stationery-office.co.uk/pa/cm 199899/cmselect/cmhaff/467/46703.htm.

"Freemasonry Under the Nazi Regime." Accessed May 3, 2010, http:// www.ushmm.org/wlc/en/article.php?ModuleId=10007187.

"Freemasons in the French Revolution." 2002. Accessed October 23, 2007, http://www.freemasonry.bcy.ca/texts/revolution.html.

Getler, Warren. 2009. "Albert Pike: The Ghost in *The Lost Symbol* Machine?" In Dan Burstein and Arne de Keijzer (eds.), *Secrets of The Lost Symbol: The Unauthorized Guide to the Mysteries Behind* The Da Vinci Code *Sequel.* New York: William Morrow/HarperCollins: 71–74.

———, and Bob Brewer. 2003. *Shadow of the Sentinel: One Man's Quest to Find the Hidden Treasure of the Confederacy.* New York: Simon & Schuster. Reprinted 2005 as *Rebel Gold.*

"Government Registry of Judiciary Masons." Autumn 1998. *Freemasonry Today* 6, http://www.freemasonrytoday.com/06/p02.php.

"Grand Lodge Responds to Select Committee Report." Autumn 1999. *Freemasonry Today* 10, http://www.freemasonrytoday.com/10/p04.php.

Halleran, Michael A. 2010. *The Better Angels of Our Nature: Freemasonry in the American Civil War.* Tuscaloosa: The University of Alabama Press.

Hamill, John. Summer 1997. "Perceptions and Realities: The Home Affairs Select Committee Report on Freemasonry in the Police and Judiciary," *Freemasonry Today* 1, http://www.freemasonrytoday.com/01/p05.php.

————. 2002. "The Current State of Freemasonry in Britain." Originally published in *Vox Lucis,* October 14, 2000, http://www.freemasonry.bcy.ca/texts/current.html.

Hammer, Emanuel F. 1958. *The Clinical Application of Projective Drawings.* Springfield, IL: Charles C. Thomas.

Hardie, James. 1818. *The New Free-Mason's Monitor; or, Masonic Guide.* New York: George Long.

Harris, Claude. 1998. *Esoteric Symbolism of the Watson-Cassoul Apron.* Accessed February 6, 2010, http://aw22.org/documents/W-C_Apron.pdf.

Henry, William E. 1956. *The Analysis of Fantasy.* New York: John Wiley.

Herodotus. 2003. *The Histories* (revised edition; Aubrey de Sélincourt, trans.; John Marincola, ed.). New York: Penguin Books. Originally composed ca. 430 BCE.

Hicks, Jimmie (ed.). July 1961. "Some Letters Concerning the Knights of the Golden Circle," *Southwestern Historical Quarterly* 65: 80–86.

Hitler, Adolf. 2009. *Mein Kampf: The Official Nazi English Translation.* n.p.: Elite Minds Inc. Originally published ca. 1937.

"Hitler and Freemasonry." Accessed May 3, 2010, http://www.freemasonry.bcy.ca/anti-masonry/hitler.html#09.

"A Hoax." 2001. Accessed February 11, 2010, http://www.freemasonry.bcy.ca/texts/taxil_confession.html.

Hodge, Susie. 2007. *The Knights Templar.* London: Anness.

Holmes, David L. 2006. *The Faiths of the Founding Fathers.* New York: Oxford University Press.

"Home Office to Pursue Register of Freemasons in the Judiciary." Autumn 2000. *Freemasonry Today* 14: 6–7.

Howarth, Stephen. 1993. *The Knights Templar*. New York: Barnes and Noble. Originally published 1982.

Humanum Genus: Encyclical of Pope Leo XIII on Freemasonry. n.d. Accessed February 12, 2010, http://www.vatican.va/holy_father/leo_xiii/encyclicals/documents/hf_l-xiii_enc_18840420_humanum-genus_en.html.

Hutchens, Rex R. 1995. *Pillars of Wisdom: The Writings of Albert Pike*. Washington, D.C.: The Supreme Council, 33°, Ancient and Accepted Scottish Rite of Freemasonry, Southern Jurisdiction, United States of America.

———. 2006. *A Bridge to Light: The Revised Standard Pike Ritual* (3rd edition; Arturo de Hoyos, editor). Washington, D.C.: The Supreme Council, 33°.

Jacob, Margaret C. 1991. *Living the Enlightenment: Freemasonry and Politics in Eighteenth-Century Europe*. New York: Oxford University Press.

———. 2006. *The Origins of Freemasonry: Facts & Fictions*. Philadelphia: University of Pennsylvania Press.

Jenkins, Ronny E. 1996. "The Evolution of the Church's Prohibition Against Catholic Membership in Freemasonry," *The Jurist* 56: 735–55.

"Judicial Review Warning Hits at Ministry of Defence 'Slur.'" Autumn 2000. *Freemasonry Today* 14: 7.

Kahler, Lisa. 1992. "Andrew Michael Ramsay and his Masonic Oration," *Heredom* 1: 19–47.

Kasser, Tim. 2002. *The High Price of Materialism*. Cambridge, MA: The MIT Press.

Kelly, Aidan A. 2007. *Inventing Witchcraft: A Case Study in the Creation of a New Religion*. Loughborough, Leicestershire, UK: Thoth Publications.

Khan, Hazrat Inayat. 1997. "The Path of Initiation and Discipleship." In H. I. Khan, *The Inner Life*. Boston: Shambhala: 99–162.

Knight, Stephen. July 2, 1978. "Why Sickert Denied Ripper Tale" (Letter to the editor). *The Sunday Times* (London): 15.

———. 1982. *Jack the Ripper: The Final Solution.* New York: HarperCollins. Originally published 1976.

———. 1986. *The Brotherhood: The Secret World of the Freemasons.* n.p.: Dorset Press. Originally published 1984.

Knoop, Douglas, and G. P. Jones. 1978. *The Genesis of Freemasonry.* London: Quatuor Coronati Lodge No. 2076. Originally published 1947.

Koltko-Rivera, Mark E. 2007. "The Transmission of Esoteric Knowledge and the Origins of Modern Freemasonry: Was Mackey *Right?*" *Heredom* 15: 179–209.

———. June 1, 2009. Part 1: The Context. (Series: The Roman Catholic Church and Freemasonry.) Entry on the blog Freemasonry: Reality, Myth, and Legend. Accessed February 11, 2010, http://themasonicblog.blogspot.com/2009/06/part-1-context-series-roman-catholic.html.

Kramnick, Isaac, ed. 1995. *The Portable Enlightenment Reader.* New York: Penguin Books.

Laurence, Richard. 2001. *The Book of Enoch.* Grantsville, UT: Archive Publishers. Originally published 1883.

"Léo Taxil's Confession." 2001. Accessed February 11, 2010, http://www.freemasonry.bcy.ca/texts/taxilconfession.html.

The Letter "Humanum Genus" of the Pope, Leo XIII, Against Freemasonry and the Spirit of the Age, April 20, 1884, and the Reply of Albert Pike, 33°, Sovereign Grand Commander of the Supreme Council, 33°, Ancient and Accepted Scottish Rite of Freemasonry, Southern Jurisdiction, USA. 1962. Washington, D.C.: The Supreme Council 33°. Originally published 1884.

"The Lie of Luciferianism." 2002. Accessed February 11, 2010, http://www.freemasonry.bcy.ca/anti-masonry/luciferianism.html.

Lundquist, John M. 1993. *The Temple: Meeting Place of Heaven and Earth.* New York: Thames and Hudson.

MacNulty, W. Kirk. 1991. *Freemasonry: A Journey Through Ritual and Symbol.* New York: Thames & Hudson.

———. 1996. "A Philosophical Background for Masonic Symbolism," *Heredom* 5: 17–34.

———. 1998. "Kabbalah and Freemasonry," *Heredom* 7: 133–205.

Macoy, Robert. 1867. *The Masonic Manual: A Pocket Companion for the Initiated* (revised edition). New York: Clark & Maynard.

"Mason's Mark, The." December 16, 2007. Accessed February 8, 2010, http://www.freemasonry.bcy.ca/grandlodge/trademark.html.

Matt, Daniel C. 1995. *The Essential Kabbalah: The Heart of Jewish Mysticism.* New York: HarperCollins.

———, ed., trans. 2004. *The Zohar: Pritzker Edition,* Vol. 1. Stanford, CA: Stanford University Press.

May, David. June 18, 1978. "Jack the Ripper 'Solution' was a Hoax, Man Confesses," *The Sunday Times* (London), p. 4.

May, Robert E. 1973. *The Southern Dream of a Caribbean Empire, 1854–1861.* Baton Rouge: Louisiana State University Press.

McIntosh, Christopher. 1998. *The Rosicrucians: The History, Mythology, and Rituals of an Esoteric Order.* San Francisco: Weiser Books.

Melzer, Ralf. 2002. "In the Eye of a Hurricane: German Freemasonry in the Weimar Republic and the Third Reich," *Heredom* 10: 203–21.

Meyer, Marvin, ed. 2007. *The Nag Hammadi Scriptures: The International Edition.* New York: HarperCollins.

Millar, Angel. 2005. *Freemasonry: A History.* San Diego, CA: Thunder Bay Press/Advantage Publishers Group.

"MoD 'Withdraws' its Instruction on Masons." Winter 2001. *Freemasonry Today* 15: 6.

Moore, Alan, and Eddie Campbell. 2006. *From Hell: Being a Melodrama in Sixteen Parts.* Marietta, GA: Top Shelf Productions. Originally published 1989.

Nagel, Georges. 1978. "The Mysteries' of Osiris in Ancient Egypt." In Joseph Campbell, ed., *The Mysteries.* Princeton, NJ: Princeton University Press: 119-134. Originally published 1944.

Naudon, Paul. 2005. *The Secret History of Freemasonry: Its Origins and Connection to the Knights Templar.* Rochester, VT: Inner Traditions.

Nibley, Hugh. 1966. "Evangelium quadraginta dierum," *Vigiliae Christianae* 20: 1–24. {In English.}

"Occult Theocrasy Notes." 2007. Accessed February 11, 2010, http://www.freemasonry.bcy.ca/anti-masonry/miller_e/occult_theocrasy_notes.html.

Otto, Walter F. 1978. "The Meaning of the Eleusinian Mysteries." In Joseph Campbell, ed., *The Mysteries.* Princeton, NJ: Princeton University Press: 14-31. Originally published 1939.

"P2 Lodge." 2010. http://www.masonicinfo.com/p2_lodge.htm.

Partner, Peter. 1990. *The Knights Templar and their Myth.* Rochester, VT: Destiny Books/Inner Traditions. Originally published 1981 by Oxford University Press; also known as *The Murdered Magicians.*

"Pentagram, The." June 18, 2007. Accessed October 10, 2007, http://freemasonry.bcy.ca/anti-masonry/pentagram.html.

"Pro Grand Master Outlines the Craft's Progress." Winter 2010. *Freemasonry Today* 9: 7.

Ravenscroft, W. 1947. "The Comacines," In *Little Masonic Library, Book II.* Richmond, VA: Macoy. Originally published 1924.

Read, Piers Paul. 1999. *The Templars.* London: Phoenix/Orion.

Reuchlin, Johann. 1993. *On the Art of the Kabbalah: De Arte Cabalistica.* Martin and Sarah Goodman, trans. Lincoln: University of Nebraska Press. Originally published 1517.

Robinson, John J. 1989. *Born in Blood: The Lost Secrets of Freemasonry.* New York: M. Evans & Co.

———. 1991. *Dungeon, Fire and Sword: The Knights Templar in the Crusades.* New York: M. Evans & Co.

Roundtree, Alton G., and Paul M. Bessel. 2006. *Out of the Shadows: The Emergence of Prince Hall Freemasonry in America, 200 Years of Endurance.* Forestville, MD: KLR Publishing.

Savedow, Steve, ed. and trans. 2000. *Sepher Rezial Hemelach: The Book of the Angel Rezial.* York Beach, ME: Weiser.

Scanlan, Matthew. Autumn 2004. "Freemasonry and the Spanish Civil War, Part II: Franco's Masonic Obsession," *Freemasonry Today* 30: 32–34, http://www.freemasonrytoday.com/30/p09.php.

Schafer, Roy. 1954. *Psychoanalytic Interpretation in Rorschach Testing.* Orlando, FL: Grune & Stratton/Harcourt Brace Jovanovich.

Schmitt, Paul. 1978. "The Ancient Mysteries in the Society of Their Time, Their Transformation and Most Recent Echoes." In Joseph Campbell, ed., *The Mysteries.* Princeton, NJ: Princeton University Press: 93-118. Originally published 1944.

Scholem, Gershom. 1974. "Merkabah Mysticism and Jewish Gnosticism." In G. Scholem, *Major Trends in Jewish Mysticism.* New York: Schocken. Originally published 1954.

———. 1978. *Kabbalah.* New York: Meridian. Originally published 1974.

"Scrap of Parchment May Absolve the Knights Templar from Their 'Crimes' after 700 Years." Winter 2008. *Freemasonry Today* 1: 18.

Stark, Rodney. 2009. *God's Battalions: The Case for the Crusades.* New York: HarperCollins.

Stevenson, David. 1988. *The Origins of Freemasonry: Scotland's Century, 1590–1710.* New York: Cambridge University Press.

———. (2001). *The First Freemasons: Scotland's Early Lodges and Their Members* (2nd edition). Edinburgh, Scotland: Grand Lodge of Scotland.

Turner, John D. 2007. "The Sethian School of Gnostic Thought." In Marvin Meyer, ed., *The Nag Hammadi Scriptures: The International Edition*: 784-789. New York: HarperCollins.

Tvedtnes, John A., Brian M. Hauglid, and John Gee, eds. 2001. *Traditions About the Early Life of Abraham*. Provo, UT: Foundation for Ancient Research and Mormon Studies/Brigham Young University.

Tyerman, Christopher. 2005. *The Crusades: A Very Short Introduction*. Oxford, England: Oxford University Press.

Van Doren, Richard W. 2004. "An Encapsulated Look at the Development of Freemasonry in the United States of America," *Heredom* 12: 327–46.

Venzi, Fabio. Winter 2010. "Freemasonry and Fascism in Italy," *Freemasonry Today* 9: 29–31, http://www.freemasonrytoday.com/51/p12.php.

Vermes, Geza, ed. and trans. 2004. *The Complete Dead Sea Scrolls in English* (revised edition). New York: Penguin Books.

Waugh, Paul. May 26, 1999. "Parliament: Select Committee—Masons 'Had Role in Stalker Case,'" *The Independent*. Accessed May 2010, http://www.independent.co.uk/news/parliament-select-committee—masons-had-role-in-stalker-case-1095975.html.

White, Michael. 1997. *Isaac Newton: The Last Sorcerer*. New York: Basic Books.

Wili, Walter. 1978. "The Orphic Mysteries and the Greek Spirit." In Joseph Campbell, ed., *The Mysteries*. Princeton, NJ: Princeton University Press: 64–92. Originally published 1944.

Yates, Frances A. 1972. *The Rosicrucian Enlightenment*. Boulder, CO: Shambhala.

———. 1991. *Giordano Bruno and the Hermetic Tradition*. Chicago: The University of Chicago Press. Originally published 1964.

Zeldis, Leon. 1998. "*The Protocols of the Elders of Zion*: Anti-Masonry and Anti-Semitism," *Heredom* 7: 89–111.

ILLUSTRATION CREDITS

Note: The term "GL-BCY" stands for "the Grand Lodge of British Columbia and Yukon, AF&AM," in Canada.

Frontispiece. Reproduced through the courtesy of GL-BCY. Accessed June 23, 2010, http://www.freemasonry.bcy.ca/texts/gmd1999/tb04.html.

Figure 4-1. Reproduced through the courtesy of GL-BCY. Accessed February 6, 2010, http://www.freemasonry.bcy.ca/images_download/star_moon_sun_book.gif.

Figure 4-2. Woodcut on page 30 of Macoy (1867).

Figure 4-3. From a Masonic magazine, *The Kneph*, September 1888, vol. 8, no. 1. Accessed February 6, 2010, http://www.freemasonry.bcy.ca/art/principal_officers_jewels/wmjewel.html.

Figure 4-4. From *The Kneph*, September 1888, vol. 8, no. 1. Accessed February 6, 2010, http://www.freemasonry.bcy.ca/art/principal_officers_jewels/swjewel.html.

Figure 4-5. From *The Kneph*, September 1888, vol. 8, no. 1. Accessed February 6, 2010, http://www.freemasonry.bcy.ca/art/principal_officers_ jewels/jwjewel.html.

Figure 4-6. From a lithograph by Fr. Schenck appearing in *The Laws and Constitutions of The Grand Lodge of Scotland of the Ancient and Honorable Fraternity of Free and Accepted Masons of Scotland* (Edinburgh, Scotland, 1848). Accessed February 6, 2010, http://www.freemasonry.bcy.ca/art/ s_and_c_schenck.html.

Figure 4-7. Detail of woodcut from Macoy (1867), p. 17.

Figure 4-8. Created by Reddi and modified by the present author; original file obtained through Wikipedia under the terms of the Creative Commons Attribution ShareAlike 3.0 License. Accessed February 6, 2010, http://en.wikipedia.org/wiki/File:Solomon%27sTempleEast.png.

Figure 4-9. Created by Reddi and modified by the present author; original file obtained through Wikipedia under the terms of the Creative Commons Attribution ShareAlike 3.0 License. Accessed February 6, 2010, http://en.wikipedia.org/wiki/File:SolomonsTemple.png.

Figure 4-10. Digitally retouched detail of woodcut from Macoy (1867), p. 77.

Figure 4-11. Reproduced through the courtesy of GL-BCY. Accessed February 6, 2010, http://www.freemasonry.bcy.ca/images_download/s&c_ leaves.gif.

Figure 4-12. Reproduced through the courtesy of GL-BCY. Accessed February 6, 2010, http://www.freemasonry.bcy.ca/art/washington_apron .html.

INDEX

ABOUT THE AUTHOR

Mark E. Koltko-Rivera, Ph.D., holds a doctoral degree in counseling psychology from New York University. For his scholarly work, he was elected a Fellow of the American Psychological Association (APA), an honor bestowed on only about 6 percent of APA's membership. He has been awarded the Margaret Gorman Early Career Award in the Psychology of Religion by Division 36 of APA. He also has been awarded the Early Career Award for Inquiry from the Society for Humanistic Psychology (Division 32 of APA). He also holds degrees from Haverford College and Fordham University.

Mark was made a Master Mason in Winter Park Lodge #239 F&AM (Florida), a 32nd-degree Freemason in the Orlando Scottish Rite Bodies (Southern Jurisdiction), and a Knight Templar in the Orlando York Rite Bodies. Having returned to his birthplace, he is pursuing affiliation with the corresponding Masonic bodies in New York City. His articles on Freemasonry have appeared in *Heredom*, the *Scottish Rite Journal*, and *The Philalethes* magazine. He writes the blog Freemasonry: Reality, Myth, and Legend (http://themasonicblog .blogspot.com/).

Mark lives with his wife, Kathleen, in Manhattan.